**INTERMEDIATE
ESL VIDEO LIBRA**

MW00761013

*CULTURE**WATCH***

Barry Tomalin

Susan Stempleski
Series Editor

PRENTICE HALL REGENTS
Englewood Cliffs, New Jersey 07632

Acquisitions Editor: **Nancy Leonhardt**
Manager of Development Services: **Louisa Hellegers**
Development Editor: **Barbara Barysh**
Editorial Production / Design Manager: **Dominick Mosco**
Editorial/Production Supervision: **Janet Johnston**
Page Composition: **Molly Pike Riccardi**
Production Coordinator: **Ray Keating**
Cover Supervisor: **Merle Krumper**
Cover Design: **Marianne Frasco**
Cover Photograph: **Comstock**
Interior Design: **Function Thru Form**
Electronic Artist: **Todd Ware**

ABC Distribution Company

Printed in the United States of America
10 9 8 7 6 5 4 3 2

ISBN 0-13-137621-7

Prentice-Hall International (UK) Limited, *London*
Prentice-Hall of Australia Pty. Limited, *Sydney*
Prentice-Hall Canada Inc., *Toronto*
Prentice-Hall Hispanoamericana, S.A., *Mexico*
Prentice-Hall of India Private Limited, *New Delhi*
Prentice-Hall of Japan, Inc., *Tokyo*
Simon & Schuster Asia Pte, Ltd., *Singapore*
Editora Prentice-Hall do Brasil, Ltda., *Rio de Janeiro*

Printed on Recycled Paper

TABLE OF CONTENTS

UNIT 1 IMMIGRATION AND RACE

UNIT 2 POETRY AND MUSIC

UNIT 3 WOMEN AND WORK

UNIT 4 MOVIES AND TECHNOLOGY

ACKNOWLEDGMENTS

Thanks to Susan Stempleski, the series editor, who has lectured all over the world and understands American culture in both its local and world contexts, and whose efficiency and organization ensure that the seams don't show!

Thanks to Barbara Barysh, the development editor, whose combination of patience, persistence, and efficiency is deeply appreciated.

Thanks finally, and far from least, to Nancy Leonhardt of Prentice Hall for making the decision to publish these marvelous cultural videos for teaching English.

Books are written only with considerable support from family and friends. Special thanks and love to Mary and Paul for their support during the preparation of this book.

INTRODUCTION TO THE SERIES

The *ABC News Intermediate ESL Video Library* is an interactive, integrated skills series designed for intermediate level adult learners of English as a second or foreign language. The series consists of five videocassettes: *BusinessWatch, CultureWatch, EarthWatch, HealthWatch,* and *InnovationWatch,* each accompanied by a student text and Instructor's Manual.

THE VIDEOS

Each videocassette consists of twelve actual broadcast segments from ABC News programs such as *World News Tonight, 20/20, The Health Show,* and *Business World.* These authentic television news reports focus on high-interest topics and expose students to natural English, spoken by a wide variety of people from diverse backgrounds and age groups. The videos are time coded and the codes are given in the textbooks so that sequences may be easily identified. The videos are also closed captioned. Teachers who have access to a closed caption decoder may wish to have their students view the captions as they carry out some of the activities. Some suggestions for activities based on closed captions are described at the end of this introduction.

THE BOOKS

Each book offers a broad range of task-based activities centering around the selected video segments. These activities provide practice in all four language skills: listening, speaking, reading, and writing. The reading material parallels or extends the news story and is drawn from several sources. The books also contain complete transcripts of the video segments. The Instructor's Manual, for each book contains an Answer Key to all the activities.

The general aims of the books are:
• To enhance comprehension of each video segment.
• To highlight and exploit specific language on the video.
• To stimulate discussion about the topics presented on the video.
• To offer authentic reading material related to the content of the video.
• To give students practice in writing clear and simple English.

SOME GENERAL SUGGESTIONS FOR TEACHING WITH VIDEO

Only recently has video moved from being something that is switched on and left to present language without the teacher's intervention to becoming a flexible resource for classroom activities. While there is no one "right way" to use video in language teaching, teachers using the materials in the *ABC News Intermediate ESL Video Library* will probably find the following general guidelines helpful:

Familiarize Yourself with the Material. Before presenting a lesson in class, view the entire sequence yourself, preferably several times and with the video transcript in hand. If time allows, try doing the activities yourself, in order to anticipate difficulties or questions your students may have.

Allow for Repeated Viewing. In order to carry out the viewing activities in the lessons efficiently, students will need to see and hear the video sequence and selected portions several times. Each viewing activity in the lessons is accompanied by a time code. Refer to these time codes and then play or replay the indicated section of the video in conjunction with the particular viewing task at hand.

Present Activities to the Students Before Viewing. Students will focus their attention more effectively on the viewing activities if you ensure that they understand the directions for each task before playing or replaying the video sequence.

Get to Know Your Equipment. Practice with the video equipment you will be using in class. The time codes on the video will help you locate the sequence to be shown and any other points you may wish to highlight.

HOW TO USE THE VIDEOS AND THE BOOKS

You can use the news stories in the *ABC News Intermediate ESL Video Library* in the order in which they are presented on the videos and in the books, or you may choose particular video segments according to the interests of your students. The video segments are not graded in terms of grammatical difficulty, and there is no artificial variation in linguistic complexity from lesson to lesson within the books. You can have students work through each exercise in a lesson, or you may choose specific activities to suit your students' needs and particular class schedule.

Each book in the *ABC News Intermediate ESL Video Library* consists of twelve 10-page lessons, each corresponding to a single news segment on the video. Every lesson is structured in the same way and has three main sections: BEFORE YOU WATCH, WHILE YOU WATCH, and AFTER YOU WATCH.

BEFORE YOU WATCH

This section contains previewing activities that prepare students to watch the video by tapping their background knowledge and stimulating interest in the topic. There are three types of activities in this section:

- **Talking Points:** These are questions designed to stimulate general discussion and elicit relevant vocabulary and background knowledge about the topic of the video segment. They also motivate students to watch the video and provide opportunities for them to exchange ideas.

- **Predicting:** These activities encourage students to think about the topic and to predict the kinds of information they think will be included on the video.

- **Key Words:** This is a vocabulary activity to introduce or review words directly related to the topic of the video.

WHILE YOU WATCH

This section contains a variety of viewing activities for students to complete while actually watching the video. The activities promote active viewing and listening and facilitate comprehension by focusing on essential features of the news story. Time codes corresponding to the appropriate section of the video are printed next to each activity. These time codes facilitate access to the relevant part of the video to be played or replayed in conjunction with the particular viewing task.

- **Getting the Main Idea:** This is a global viewing activity in which students watch the entire video segment and answer questions about key ideas (the who, what, where, why, when, and how) of the segment.

The remaining activities in the WHILE YOU WATCH section take students through the video bit by bit to focus on more specific information. In order to carry out these activities efficiently students are asked to watch and hear particularly relevant sections of the video again to gain a detailed understanding of the news story. The activities used and the order in which they are presented vary, but they include a combination of several of the following types:

- **Checking Your Predictions:** Students watch the video and check to see if their predictions about the content of the video were correct.

- **What's Missing?:** This is a listening cloze. Students listen to a portion of the video segment and fill in the missing words in a section of the video transcript.

- **True or False?:** Students watch a section of the video and indicate whether the statements in the exercise are true or false. Students are additionally challenged by being asked to change the false sentences to make them true.

- **Checking What You Hear:** Students watch the video and check particular details that are mentioned on the video.

- **Listening for Details:** Students watch the video and circle the correct answers to a series of multiple-choice type questions.

- **Checking What You See:** This activity encourages students to pay close attention to visual information presented on the video. Students watch the video and check the images they actually see.

- **Notetaking:** Students watch the video and take brief notes on the answers to a series of *Wh-* questions focusing on specific details.

- **Information Match:** This is a matching exercise. Students watch the video and match the names of people, places, or things with related information.

- **Putting Events in Order:** This is a sequencing activity. Students watch the video segment and number a series of events in the order in which they are presented on the video.

- **Making Inferences:** Students watch the video and are asked to reach logical conclusions, based on the facts presented in the news story.

- **Identifying What You See:** Students watch selected portions of the video and identify what they see by writing a brief description.

- **Making True Sentences:** This is a matching exercise in which students write true sentences about the video by combining sentence stems and endings.

- **Who's Who?:** Students watch the video and check the sentences that apply to different people who are interviewed or shown on the video.

AFTER YOU WATCH

This section contains postviewing activities related to the topic of the video. The activities stimulate language use and encourage students to integrate information from the video. This section always contains the following six activity types:

- **Language Point:** In this activity, a selected language function or grammar point from the video is highlighted for further practice.

- **Vocabulary Check:** This activity reviews idioms, colloquial expressions, and other words or phrases used on the video.

- **Discussion:** These are questions that encourage students to relate the information on the video to their own lives and/or the situation in their own countries.

- **Role Play:** This activity provides students with an opportunity to use the information and language they have acquired while working on the video in a freer practice stage.

- **Reading:** This activity offers authentic reading material — such as magazine articles — related to the content of the video.

- **Writing:** In these activities, students are encouraged to integrate and use information from the video to prepare letters, short news articles, and other original documents.

SOME SUGGESTIONS FOR USING CLOSED CAPTIONS

As mentioned above, an additional feature of the videos in the *ABC News Intermediate ESL Video Library* is that all the video segments, with the exception of those from *The Health Show* and *Business World*, are closed captioned. If you have access to a closed captioned decoder (or a television with the new decoder chip) you may wish to open up the captions and have your students do the following variations of some of the activity types in the books:

- **Key Words:** Have students read the captions and call out "Stop!" when they see one of the key words in the captions. Use the pause button to stop the video at that point, and have students suggest the meaning of the word as it is used in the segment.

- **Checking Your Predictions:** Instead of having students *listen for* the information which they have predicted, they can be asked to *read* the captions to locate the relevant information.

- **What's Missing?:** As a variation of this activity, students can be asked to fill in the blanks (using any words that make sense) *before* watching the video. Students then watch the video, and read the captions to check their answers.

- **Vocabulary Check:** As in the variation of the Key Words activity just described, students can be asked to read the captions and indicate when they *see* the idioms, colloquial expressions, and other words or phrases highlighted in the Vocabulary Check.

These are just a few ways in which the closed captions on the segments can be used to enhance language learning. Allow your imagination to come up with ideas. In situations in which a closed caption decoder is not available, students can carry out similar activities by using the video transcripts in the back of the book.

SUGGESTIONS FOR STUDENTS WORKING WITHOUT A TEACHER

Language learners differ from one another in many ways. If you are learning English without a teacher, you should use the materials in the *ABC News Intermediate ESL Video Library* in the way that is most suitable to *you* and *your* situation. However, your work will probably be more pleasant and productive if you do the following:

- Follow the plan of each lesson.

- Read the directions to each exercise carefully.

- Use the Answer Key only when you have to — and that should be after you have completed the exercise. The Answer Key is in the Instructor's Manual.

- If an exercise does not have clear-cut answers in the Answer Key, try to do the exercise with another person: a native speaker or someone at your own level of English.

- Use the transcripts of the video segments to study the language used on the video in detail. The transcripts are printed in the back of the book.

- Set realistic goals for yourself as you work on the lessons. As with learning many other things, the key to successful language learning is to do a small amount of work regularly and frequently. If doing one lesson a week is too much, try doing one over two weeks.

- If you have a closed caption decoder, you may find it helpful to follow along with the speakers and read the words on the screen.

Finally, enjoy improving your English with the *ABC News Intermediate ESL Video Library!*

Segment 1
Steven Briganti, Ellis Island Restorer

From: *World News Tonight,* 9/7/90
Begin: 00:34
Length: 4:81

BEFORE YOU WATCH

TALKING POINTS

Work in groups. Discuss your answers to the following questions.

1. Were you born in the country in which you are now living? If not, where were you born?

2. Were your parents born in the country in which they are now living? If not, where were they born? Why did they leave their home country?

3. What are some reasons that people have for immigrating to a new country?

4. Do many people enter your country as immigrants? If so, from what countries do they usually come? Why do they immigrate to your country?

PREDICTING

The video is about Steven Briganti, the man responsible for restoring Ellis Island, an important monument to American immigration. What do you think you will see and hear on the video? Write down three items under each of the headings that follow. Then compare your answers with those of another student.

SIGHTS	**WORDS**
(things you expect to see)	(words you expect to hear)

1. _____   _____

2. _____   _____

3. _____   _____

KEY WORDS

The *italicized* words in the sentences below will help you understand the video. Study the sentences. Then match the words with the meanings.

1. Thousands of *refugees* began to flee the country as a result of the war.
2. She works for the Ford *Foundation*.
3. The building has been *rededicated* as the War Memorial Museum.
4. He felt great *anxiety* when he heard about his daughter's accident.
5. They left their country to escape *oppression*.
6. The first astronauts were *pioneers* in space travel.
7. U.S. Government controls on *immigration* have changed over the years.
8. The sinking boat was *abandoned* by the fishermen.
9. He was *deported* from the United States.
10. Our country is a *sanctuary* for people of different political opinions.

1. _h_ *refugees*
2. _i_ *foundation*
3. _a_ *rededicated*
4. _f_ *anxiety*
5. _d_ *oppression*
6. _g_ *pioneers*
7. _j_ *immigration*
8. _b_ *abandoned*
9. _c_ *deported*
10. _e_ *sanctuary*

a. renamed in a formal ceremony

b. left completely and finally

c. legally sent out of a country

d. cruel or unfair treatment of a group of people

e. a place of safety

f. worry caused by uncertainty about the future

g. people who are among the first to go to a new place or do a new thing

h. people forced to leave their country because of war or their political or religious beliefs

i. an organization that provides money for a special purpose

j. the coming of people into a country in order to live there

WHILE YOU WATCH

GETTING THE MAIN IDEA

Watch the news report and listen for the answers to the following questions. Take brief notes on the answers. Then compare your answers with those of another student.

00:42–
05:09

Who has done **what**? **Where**?
When was this done? **Why** was it important to do?

Who?	
What?	
Where?	
When?	
Why?	

CHECKING YOUR PREDICTIONS

Look at the lists you made in the PREDICTING exercise on page 2. Watch the video and check (✔) the items that you actually see and hear.

00:42–
05:09

WHAT'S MISSING?

Listen to Peter Jennings's introduction to the news report. Fill in the missing words.

00:48–
01:44

Peter Jennings: Finally this evening, our Person of the Week. There has been a great deal of attention paid this week to all of the (1) _____ created by the situation in Iraq and Kuwait. Hundreds of thousands of people (2) _____ because they are suddenly no longer able to make a (3) _____ , even worse, (4) _____ that they may be trapped in the middle of a (5) _____ — which reminded us that this weekend millions of Americans will have an opportunity to contemplate the refugees in their past.

* * *

Steven Briganti is responsible for making sure we know. Briganti is the guiding force at the (6) _____ that has renovated and restored the Ellis Island Immigration Center in the (7) _____ of New York. This weekend it will be rededicated as the Ellis Island Immigration Museum, a monument to the greatest (8) _____ of human beings in modern history.

CHECKING WHAT YOU HEAR AND SEE

01:43–
01:56

Watch the next part of the news report. Check (✔) the feelings or expressions of feelings that Professor David Reimers mentions in connection with Ellis Island.

1. ❑ smiles
2. ❑ romance
3. ❑ excitement
4. ❑ hysteria
5. ❑ sadness

6. ❑ tears
7. ❑ anxiety
8. ❑ tiredness
9. ❑ laughter
10. ❑ fear

TRUE OR FALSE?

01:57–
02:21

Watch the video. Are the following statements about Steven Briganti *true* or *false*? Write **T** (true) or **F** (false). Make the false statements true by changing one or two words.

1. F Steven Briganti's family came to the United States from Spain.
2. T Steven Briganti has a deep feeling for Ellis Island.
3. F His four grandparents came through Ellis Island.
4. T His mother also came through Ellis Island.
5. F Steven Briganti was born in India.
6. F He was raised in New York City.
7. F His grandmother told him stories about Ellis Island.
8. F As a child, he paid a lot of attention to Ellis Island.

LISTENING FOR DETAILS

Watch the video again. Circle the correct answers.

02:22–04:53

1. In what year did the Great Immigration Hall at Ellis Island first open?
   a. 1872.
   b. 1882.
   c. 1892.

2. By 1945, how many immigrants had passed through Ellis Island?
   a. 70 million.
   b. 17 million.
   c. 7 million.

3. Where did most of these immigrants come from?
   a. Europe.
   b. South America.
   c. China and the Far East.

4. Why did these immigrants leave their home countries?
   a. They wanted to escape oppression and hunger.
   b. They were looking for more opportunity.
   c. Both a and b.

5. In the late 1920s, how many immigrants were processed at Ellis Island?
   a. 5,000 a day.
   b. 5,000 a week.
   c. 5,000 a month.

6. By what decade had the great wave of European immigration to the U.S. subsided (decreased)?
   a. The 1930s.
   b. The 1940s.
   c. The 1950s.

7. What happened to Ellis Island in 1954?
   a. The island was sold and used as a parking lot.
   b. The Immigration Center was closed down and abandoned.
   c. Both a and b.

8. When did Steven Briganti and the Ellis Island Foundation start to raise money for the project?
   a. In 1964.
   b. In 1974.
   c. In 1984.

9. What did Steven Briganti want to preserve about Ellis Island?
   a. The good memories.
   b. The bad memories.
   c. Both a and b.
10. According to Steven Briganti, what does Ellis Island symbolize?
   a. Hope and opportunity.
   b. Illness and deportation.
   c. Both a and b.

NOTETAKING

Watch the video again and take brief notes on the answers to the following questions. Then compare your notes with those of another student.

03:13–
05:09

1. What country did Bertha Devlin emigrate from? How old was she then?

   _____

2. What was the Great Immigration Hall like when she arrived?

   _____

3. Why were some immigrants marked with an "X"?

   _____

4. What happened to those immigrants who were marked with an "X"?

   _____

5. What other great American monument did Steven Briganti restore before he began working on the Ellis Island project?

   _____

6. According to Peter Jennings, what two basic values does America symbolize?

   _____

AFTER YOU WATCH

LANGUAGE POINT: TALKING ABOUT EVENTS IN THE PAST

Two ways to talk about past events in English are: the *simple past* meaning *then* or *at that time*, and the *present perfect*, meaning *since that time*. Study these examples:

Simple past: Bertha Devlin *came* to the U.S. from Ireland in 1923.
Present perfect: Bertha Devlin *has lived* in the U.S. since 1923.

Complete the paragraphs below. Use the simple past or the present perfect tense of the verbs in parentheses, whichever is more appropriate. The first one has been done for you.

The Great Immigration Hall on Ellis Island first _opened_ in 1892.
(1. open)

From 1892 through the late 1920s, about 5,000 immigrants a day

Arrived at Ellis Island. Since he was child, Steven Briganti
(2. arrive)

Has had a deep feeling for Ellis Island. Many years ago, his own
(3. have)

parents came through the Immigration Center from Italy. When
(4. come)

he was a child, his mother told him a lot of stories about Ellis
(5. tell)

Island. In the 1980s, Steven Briganti began to work on the Ellis
(6. begin)

Island project. Since that time, he has continued to work for the Ellis
(7. continue)

Island Foundation. Before he began to work for the foundation, he

was in charge of refurbishing the Statue of Liberty. In 1990, the
(8. be)

Ellis Island Immigration Museum opened its doors to the public.
(9. open)

Since then, thousands of people have visited this important monument.
(10. visit)

VOCABULARY CHECK

The following excerpts are from the video. What do the *italicized* words and expressions mean? Circle the correct answer.

1. . . . people fleeing because they are suddenly no longer able to *make a living.*

   a. have an interesting life   c. reach the place where they live

   b. stay alive and healthy   (d.) earn enough money to live properly

2. Through the late 1920s, 5,000 people a day were *herded in* and processed in Ellis Island's Great Hall.
    a. pushed through like cattle
    b. given food
    c. looked after
    d. robbed

3. The place was *packed*. There was no room to move around.
    a. decorated
    b. empty
    c. crowded
    d. closed

4. In the three decades since, it *went very much to seed*.
    a. became a large garden
    b. was made a lot bigger
    c. was visited by a lot of sightseers
    d. got into a very bad condition

5. Briganti and the Ellis Island Foundation began to *raise money*.
    a. borrow or ask for money
    b. lend or give away money
    c. lose money
    d. save money

6. If . . . *shortness of breath was detected*, they were marked with an "X" and often deported.
    a. slow breathing
    b. difficulty breathing
    c. excited behavior
    d. unpleasant breath

7. Steven Briganti is very pleased with the way the restoration *turned out*.
    a. ended up
    b. started to go
    c. continued
    d. was given to someone else

8. Before he became the guardian of this Ellis Island project, he was in charge of *refurbishing* the Statue of Liberty.
    a. raising money to pay for
    b. writing the history of
    c. rebuilding
    d. cleaning and redecorating

DISCUSSION

Work in groups. Discuss your answers to the following questions.

1. In your opinion, what was the most interesting thing about the news report?

2. Would you like to visit the Ellis Island Immigration Museum? Why or why not?

3. The Ellis Island Immigration Museum is an important historical monument in the United States. Describe an important historical monument in your country. What is its name? Where is it located? What does it commemorate?

4. Do you know anyone who has immigrated to your country? If so, tell the class what you know about the person. Where did the person emigrate from? When did he/she immigrate to your country? Why did he/she emigrate there?

ROLE PLAY

Work in pairs. One student will be the interviewer. The other student will play the role of Steven Briganti. Read the situation and role descriptions below and decide who will play each role. After a ten-minute preparation, begin the role play.

SITUATION: **A Radio Interview**

> A radio program called "Inside America" has invited Steven Briganti to talk about the Ellis Island Restoration project.

ROLE DESCRIPTION: **Interviewer**

> You are the interviewer for "Inside America." Prepare a list of questions to ask Steven Briganti about the Ellis Island project.

ROLE DESCRIPTION: **Steven Briganti**

> You are Steven Briganti. Be prepared to answer questions about the Ellis Island project.

READING

Read the passage below to find out about national groups that took part in the great wave of European immigration to America. Then answer the questions that follow.

THE IMMIGRANTS

Immigrants to America late in the 19th and early in the 20th century came from all over Europe — from Germany, Italy, France, England, Ireland and Scotland, Russia, Hungary, Czechoslovakia, and Poland. Their names and where they came from are reflected today in American family names and place names such as "Little Italy" in New York. Sociologists talk about "push" factors and "pull" factors that cause immigration. The "pull" factors were the opportunities to earn money and have a better life in America, despite the discomfort of the ocean voyage and the risk of the unknown. The "push" factors were the very difficult living conditions for many Europeans, especially those in farming communities. In Ireland, for example, the great potato famine of 1845 drove many (FAHEM)

emigrants to America. Many of those people's descendants are among the most famous names in America today.

More than two and half million people emigrated from Poland. Some of them were called <u>za chelbem</u> or "for bread" immigrants. They didn't want to settle permanently in America. They intended to work, save money, and then return to Poland. One twenty-six-year-old immigrant to New York to earn money to buy land or to rent a flour mill in Poland. Another Pole was only twenty-three. He felt he had no hope in his own country. He owned a small farm worth very little money and had a large family. No matter how hard he worked they would always be very poor in Poland. He hoped he could earn more money and find a better life for his family in America.

1. Name three countries from which immigrants came to settle in America.

   _____

2. What is the "push" factor?

   _____

3. What is the "pull" factor?

   _____

4. What happened in 1845 to drive Irish emigrants to America?

   _____

5. The reading describes two immigrants and their reasons for wanting to go to America. Complete the following chart with information about those two immigrants.

   _____

	First Immigrant	Second Immigrant
Nationality		
Age		
Reason for wanting to go to America		
Planned to settle in America? (Answer *yes* or *no.*)		

WRITING
Complete one of the following activities.

1. Imagine you are one of the immigrants just described in the excerpt from *The Polish Americans*. You've immigrated to America and have just arrived at Ellis Island. Write a letter (100–150 words) to a relative or friend back home in Poland. Describe your arrival in America and your experience at Ellis Island.

2. You work for the Ellis Island Foundation. You are preparing a press release for a newspaper, announcing the reopening of the Ellis Island Immigration Center as the Ellis Island Immigration Museum. Write 150–200 words describing Ellis Island: what it was used for in the past, Steven Briganti's role in its restoration, and why Ellis Island is an important American monument.

Segment 2
Spike Lee on His Movie
Do the Right Thing

From: *World News Tonight*, 7/7/89
Begin: 05:20
Length: 5:16

BEFORE YOU WATCH

TALKING POINTS

Work in groups. Discuss your answers to the following questions.

1. Are there different racial groups in your country? If so, what are they? Are relations between different racial groups a problem in your country? Explain your answer.

2. Have you ever been discriminated against (treated unfairly) because of your race, religion, or culture? If so, describe your experience.

3. In a country, such as the United States, where many different racial groups live together, what special problems does the country face?

4. What can be done to encourage people of different races to get along better?

PREDICTING

The video is about Spike Lee's movie *Do the Right Thing*. Predict the kinds of information you think will be included in the video.

1. _____

2. _____

3. _____

4. _____

KEY WORDS

The *italicized* words in the sentences below will help you understand the video. Study the sentences. Then write your own definition of each word.

1. Movies about race, politics, or religion are often *controversial*.

   controversial: Strong opinion

2. In places where different races live together, people are often concerned about *race relations*.

   race relations: The kind of Relation that They have

3. She described some *incidents* of racial discrimination in her country.

   incidents: When Something Happens.

4. I can't find my other *sneaker*, so I'll have to wear my shoes.

   sneaker: Special Shoes for Do Mercise

5. There are a lot of stores and restaurants in this *block*.

   block: Street.

6. She lives in a *brownstone* in Brooklyn, New York.

   brownstone: Specel kind of building

7. The owner lost a lot of business because of the *boycott* of his store.

   (?) *boycott:* When The people Decide dunt buy in the store

8. Black customers said the owner of the shop was guilty of *racism*.

   racism: When Somebody is Roist

9. He enjoys listening to rap music on his *boom box*.

   boom box: A Big Radio or A Big Stereo.

10. The *cops* arrived and made a lot of arrests.

    cops: The pulice

11. The police were called in to control the *riots*.

    (riots) *riots:* people out of control

12. Crimes involving *violence* are a serious problem in some big cities.

    violence: Hitting someone.

WHILE YOU WATCH

GETTING THE MAIN IDEA

Watch the report and listen for the answers to the following questions. Take brief notes on the answers. Then compare your answers with those of another student.

05:26–
10:30

Who is Spike Lee?

What is his film *Do the Right Thing* about?

Why did he make the film?

How have critics responded to the film?

Who?	
What?	
Why?	
How?	

CHECKING YOUR PREDICTIONS

Look at your answers to the PREDICTING exercise on pages 11 and 12. Watch the video again and check (✔) the kinds of information that are actually included on the video.

05:26–
10:30

WHAT'S MISSING?

Listen to Peter Jennings's introduction to the report. Fill in the missing words.

05:31–
5:54

Peter Jennings: Finally this evening, our Person of the Week. So many people are talking about him this week. The film which he (1) _____ and (2) _____ and wrote and starred in has just (3) _____ at movie houses all across the country, and all the (4) _____ can't hurt at the box office. But he will be particularly (5) _____ because he's made an (6) _____ film, a (7) _____ film, one which may make a (8) _____.

NOTE TAKING

05:55–
10:14

Watch the video and take brief notes on the answers to the following questions. Then compare your notes with those of another student.

1. What does Spike Lee believe it is his job as a filmmaker to do?

   _____

2. What does he think a lot more people will do because of his film?

   _____

3. What issues does the film *Do the Right Thing* deal with?

   _____

4. What point does the film make?

   _____

5. According to Spike Lee, what simple question does *Do the Right Thing* ask?

   _____

WHO'S WHO?

06:15–
09:22

What are the facts about the characters in *Do the Right Thing*? Look at the chart below. Then watch the video and check (✔) the appropriate boxes.

Who . . . ?	Sal	Buggin' Out	Radio Raheem	a young white man
1. owns a pizzeria in the neighborhood	✔			
2. wheeled a bicycle over someone's sneaker				✔
3. was wearing the sneaker		✔		
4. owns a brownstone in the neighborhood				✔
5. organizes a black boycott of the pizzeria		✔		
6. refuses to turn down his boom box in the pizzeria			✔	
7. destroys the radio and calls someone "nigger"	✔			
8. is killed by a policeman			✔	

LISTENING FOR DETAILS

Watch the video. Circle the correct answers.

07:29–08:32

1. Spike Lee says his movie is
   a. like *ET*.
   b. like real life.
   c. like Walt Disney.

2. Spike Lee was born in _____ and grew up in _____
   a. Maryland . . . Brooklyn.
   b. Atlanta . . . Brooklyn.
   c. Brooklyn . . . Atlanta.

3. According to Peter Jennings, some critics think that the characters in Spike Lee's film are
   a. humorous and heart-warming.
   b. intellectually deep.
   c. unsophisticated and immature.

4. According to Stanley Crouch, Spike Lee
   a. has an informed, mature view of racism.
   b. represents an intellectual level that is not very deep.
   c. has appeared on MTV.

5. According to David Ansen, Spike Lee
   a. is trying to start a riot.
   b. wants people to start talking about racism.
   c. represents an uninformed view of racism.

TRUE OR FALSE?

Watch the video. Are the following statements *true* or *false*? Write **T** (true) or **F** (false). Make the false statements true by changing one or two words.

08:33–10:07

1. __F__ Spike Lee believes that in America the same value is put on a black life as on a white life.

2. __F__ Spike Lee thinks the reviews of his film talk too little about the destruction of Sal's Pizzeria.

3. __F__ Spike Lee thinks the murder of Radio Raheem in the film is a non-racist murder.

4. __T__ Spike Lee is criticized by people who believe his film might cause violence.

5. __T__ Spike Lee wants people to discuss racism.

6. __T__ Spike Lee worries that black and white people can't live together.

LANGUAGE POINT: RELATIVE PRONOUNS

Study these sentences:

> Spike Lee, *who* produced *Do the Right Thing*, is 32 years old.
> The movie *which* he made is controversial.
> The story involves black and white characters, all of *whom* live in the same neighborhood.
> The man *whose* boom box was destroyed is named Radio Raheem.

The following excerpts are from the video. Fill in the blanks with *who*, *which*, *whom*, or *whose*. Then watch the video again and check your answers.

1. The film _____ he produced and directed and wrote and starred in has just opened at movie houses all across the country.

2. He's made an unusual film, a controversial film, one _____ may make a difference.

3. Sal, _____ built and owns Sal's Pizzeria . . . and his two sons, one of _____ can hardly wait to escape what he regards as a totally hostile environment. . .

4. A young white man accidentally wheels his bicycle over the brand new sneaker of the neighborhood's most provocative troublemaker, _____ goes by the name of "Buggin' Out."

5. Spike Lee is 32, "only 32" to some of his critics, _____ find his portrayal of both the neighborhood and its characters in this film unsophisticated and immature.

6. Do we have to discuss racism on an MTV level of intellectual depth, _____ is what Spike Lee represents?

7. Lee is criticized by those _____ believe he has thoughtlessly or calculatingly risked inciting real violence.

8. And so we choose Spike Lee, _____ film has prompted us to think about the great black American poet, the late Langston Hughes, _____ wondered in one poem, "What happens to the dream deferred?"

VOCABULARY CHECK

The *italicized* words are used on the video. Cross out the word or phrase that does not have a similar meaning to the word or phrase in *italics*.

1. *contentedly*   happily   comfortably   regretfully

2. *hostile*   favorable   opposed   unfriendly

3. *provocative*   irritating   comforting   annoying

4. *portrayal*   entrance   representation   illustration

5. *unsophisticated*   simple   artless   knowledgeable

6. *immature*   full-grown   young   undeveloped

7. *breakdown*   failure   recovery   collapse

8. *bully*   shy person   tough guy   thug

9. *dreaded*   terrible   delightful   greatly feared

10. *despite*   aside from   apart from   including

IDIOMATIC EXPRESSIONS

The following excerpts are from the video. What do the *italicized* expressions mean? Circle the correct answer.

1. . . . the neighborhood's most provocative troublemaker, who *goes by* the name of "Buggin' Out."
   a. uses
   b. remembers
   c. repeats
   d. rejects

2. He doesn't want to *let anybody off the hook* too easily.
   a. catch anyone
   b. fish for anyone
   c. throw anyone into the water
   d. free anyone of responsibility

3. All they do is *harp upon* the destruction of Sal's Pizzeria.
   a. stop talking about
   b. keep talking about
   c. play music about
   d. sing about

4. Sal *loses his cool.*
   a. begins to feel hot
   b. gets angry
   c. misplaces his air conditioner
   d. can't find his refrigerator

5. . . . and *all hell breaks loose.*
   a. there is a minor problem
   b. all problems disappear
   c. there is a lot of swearing
   d. a riot begins

MATCHING VERBS, NOUNS, AND MEANINGS

The verbs and nouns in the boxes below used in the video. Which verbs and nouns are used together? What do they mean? Match the verbs, nouns, and meanings. The first one has been done for you.

Verbs	Nouns	Meanings
1. touch	consciences	emphasize an idea
2. do	debate	refer to a sensitive topic
3. make	violence	increase people's awareness
4. prick	a point	sell goods or provide a service
5. incite	a nerve	start discussion
6. ignite	business	encourage harmful behavior

DISCUSSION

Work in groups. Discuss your answers to the following questions.

1. Some critics say Spike Lee was right to make *Do the Right Thing*. Some say he wasn't. From what you know of the film, do you think Spike Lee was right or wrong to make the film?

2. In the film Sal calls people "nigger" and "all hell breaks loose." Why is "nigger" such a "dreaded word"? What are acceptable ways of referring to black people? white people? people who practice the religion of Judaism? people who speak Spanish? people who practice the Islamic religion? homosexuals? people in other racial, ethnic, or religious groups?

3. We all have stories about the first time we met someone of another race, nationality, or social group, either at school, in our home town, or on a trip. Describe such an incident from your own life.

ROLE PLAY

Work in groups of three. One student will play the role of the chairperson, the second will play the role of the member of community A, the third will play the role of the member of community B. Read the situation and role descriptions that follow and decide who will play each role. After a ten-minute preparation, begin the discussion.

THE SITUATION: **A Radio Discussion**

A local radio program called "Equal Time" has invited leaders of two different ethnic communities in your city or town to talk about problems between the two communities.

ROLE DESCRIPTION: **Chairperson**

Make up a list of questions to identify any problems between community A and community B and the ways relations between the two communities might be improved. Your job is to introduce the topic and the guests, and then run the discussion, getting answers from each guest.

ROLE DESCRIPTION: **Member of Community A**

You are a member of the _____ (your choice) community. Make up a list of problems you see between the two communities and the ways you think relations between the two communities might be improved.

ROLE DESCRIPTION: **Member of Community B**

You are a member of the _____ (your choice) community. Make up a list of problems you see between the two communities and the ways you think relations between the two communities might be improved.

READING

Read the article *Black and White in America* to find out about the history of race relations in the United States. Then answer the questions that follow.

BLACK AND WHITE IN AMERICA

The story of black Americans is rooted in the experience of slavery. Throughout the 18th century, hundreds of thousands of Africans were brought to America to work as slaves, in cruel and inhuman conditions, in the cotton fields and on the tobacco plantations of the South.

The U.S. outlawed slave importation in 1808, but the slave trade continued illegally until 1860, when Abraham Lincoln was elected President on an anti-slavery platform. Slavery was a major cause of the Civil War, which broke out after seven Southern states seceded from the Union in 1861 and set up the "Confederate States of America." In 1863 Lincoln issued the Emancipation Proclamation that freed "all slaves in areas still in rebellion." However, slavery was not completely abolished until 1865, the year the Civil War ended with the Confederate Army surrender.

After the war, many black people went to live and work in Northern cities. Although there were no longer any slaves, the two races lived apart in the South, where whites enjoyed a higher standard of living than blacks. In 1954 the U.S. outlawed segregation, but discrimination against blacks continued in fact. The Civil Rights movement in the 1960's, led by Dr. Martin Luther King, Jr., demanded equal rights for black Americans. In 1964 the Civil Rights Bill, banning discrimination in voting, jobs, and other areas of American life, was passed. Four years later, King was assassinated in Memphis, Tennessee.

Because of this history, there is still tension between blacks and whites in many parts of the U.S. In some cases, this is due to very different standards of living between the communities. Many black Americans are caught in a "poverty trap" of low-paid jobs and live in poorer parts of the "inner cities," where violence and high crime rates are a fact of life.

The black community has made a fundamental contribution in all walks of American life — politics, government, the military, the arts, sports, and academia. Nevertheless, while millions of black Americans graduate from college, have high-paid jobs, and are leading members of American society, "inner city" blacks are an angry, high-profile minority and a continuing reminder of America's past. This is what Spike Lee's film *Do the Right Thing* addresses.

1. Where did the ancestors of most of the black Americans come from? When did most of them arrive in America?

   _____

2. Where did most of them originally live and work in the United States?

   _____

3. What was the name of the war that ended slavery in the United States, and when was it fought?

   _____

4. When was segregation outlawed in the U.S.? When was discrimination outlawed?

   _____

5. What issue does Spike Lee's film address?

   _____

WRITING

Complete one of the following activities.

1. Use the information on the video to write a 150–200 summary of *Do the Right Thing*. Identify the main characters and say what happens in the story.

2. You are an author. Think of a community relations problem in your own city or country. In groups, discuss a possible story that illustrates the problem. Then write a 150-word proposal summarizing your idea for a short story, a book, or a film.

Segment 3
Those Terrible Taxis!

From: *20/20*, 3/30/90
Begin: 10:40
Length: 7:27

BEFORE YOU WATCH

TALKING POINTS

Work in groups. Discuss your answers to the following questions.

1. How often do you take a taxicab? Why do you take a cab rather than another form of transportation?

2. Do you think taxis in your city are expensive, cheap, or reasonable?

3. What kind of person becomes a taxi driver?

4. In general, which are the most common characteristics of taxi drivers you have met ?

honest	rude	helpful
dishonest	polite	unhelpful

PREDICTING

Based on the title of the video segment, *Those Terrible Taxis*, what do you think you will see on the video? Choose from the scenes listed on the following page and check the appropriate boxes. Then compare your answers with those of another student.

1. ☒ a crash
2. ☒ a street argument
3. ❏ a training center
4. ☒ a fight

5. ☒ an angry passenger in the street
6. ☒ a court
7. ❏ an instructional tour
8. ❏ something else

KEY WORDS

The *italicized* words in the sentences below will help you understand the video. Study the sentences. Then match the words with the meanings.

1. I'm so happy to be away from that *hellhole*!
2. He's the *stereotype* of an army officer.
3. The passenger asked the taxi driver for his *hack number*.
4. She told him that she was an *immigrant* from Russia.
5. The companies formed a *cartel* to prevent competition and to control prices.
6. She took a *yellow cab* to her office downtown.
7. Before you can buy a taxicab in New York, you have to own a *medallion*.
8. He's working as a *cabbie* in New York City.
9. The woman gave the cab driver a dollar *tip*.
10. The government class went on a *field trip* to the mayor's office.

1. __d__ *hellhole*

a. a person from a foreign country who enters another country to make his home there

2. __j__ *stereotype*

b. a taxi driver

3. __h__ *hack number*

c. a tour to study school subjects in real life

4. __a__ *immigrant*

d. a very unpleasant place

5. __f__ *cartel*

e. an officially registered New York taxi

6. __e__ *yellow cab*

f. a combination of business organizations

7. __i__ *medallion*

g. a small gift of money for services provided

8. __b__ *cabbie* (cab driver)

h. a series of digits that identifies a taxi driver

9. __g__ *tip*

i. a round metal disc which identifies a registered taxi in New York City

10. __c__ *field trip*

j. a fixed idea or image (often wrong) of a group of people or a country

WHILE YOU WATCH

GETTING THE MAIN IDEA

Watch the news report and listen for the answers to the following questions. Take brief notes on the answers. Then compare your answers with those of another student.

10:47–
18:10

> **Who** is doing **what**, **where**?
>
> **Why** and **how** are they doing this?

Who?	
What?	
Where?	
Why?	
How?	

CHECKING YOUR PREDICTIONS

Look at the items you checked in the PREDICTING exercise on page 22. Watch the video and circle the things that you actually see.

10:47–
18:10

WHAT'S MISSING? home

Listen to John Stossel's introduction to the news report. Fill in the missing words.

11:42–
12:15

John Stossel: Okay. You've made it to (1) _____ _____.

You've survived the (2) _____ , but now you've really got

something to worry about: the (3) New York _____ _____ .

You've heard the stories; they're rude, reckless. These are tough

(4) _____ New Yorkers who know all the tricks. They'll cheat

you on the (5) _____ , maybe drop you off at some hellhole,

miles from your hotel. Well, some of the stories are true. What

you might not know is that when (6) _____ _____ live up to

the vicious stereotype, we (7) _____ can file a (8) _____

that'll force them to come here.

CHECKING WHAT YOU HEAR

12:16–
13:09

Watch the next part of the news report. Check (✔) the complaints the *passengers* mention.

1. ❑ refused to let me out
2. ❑ overcharged me
3. ❑ wasn't courteous to me
4. ❑ didn't keep the cab clean

5. ❑ didn't speak english
6. ❑ didn't stop for me
7. ❑ drove too fast
8. ❑ wouldn't go to exact destination

LISTENING FOR DETAILS *Home*

12:30–
13:55

Watch the video. Circle the correct answers.

1. The passengers made their complaints in
   a. a police station.
   b. a taxi rank.
   c. a special taxi court.

2. Taxi drivers say they sometimes refuse to take passengers because
   a. the area is dangerous.
   b. they want to go home.
   c. they don't like the passenger's face.

3. Most New York City taxi drivers
   a. are native New Yorkers.
   b. come from all over the world.
   c. come from other parts of the United States.

4. You may own a yellow cab if
   a. you live in the United States.
   b. you have driven a cab before.
   c. you own a medallion.

TRUE OR FALSE? *Home*

13:51–
14:30

Watch the video. Which sentence in each pair is true? Check the appropriate boxes.

1. a. ❑ Native New Yorkers can't drive taxis because there are too many immigrants.
   b. ❑ Native New Yorkers don't want to drive taxis.

2. a. ❑ To drive a taxi in a New York you need a medallion.
   b. ❑ To drive a taxi in New York you don't need a medallion.

3. a. ❑ You get a medallion from a cab company that already has one.

   b. ❑ You get a medallion from the licensing bureau.

4. a. ❑ A new medallion costs $130,000.

   b. ❑ A new medallion costs $13,000.

5. a. ❑ New drivers rent medallions for $80 a day.

   b. ❑ New drivers rent cabs for $80 a day.

6. a. ❑ It's easy to make money by driving a cab.

   b. ❑ It's very difficult to make money by driving a cab.

NOTETAKING

Watch the next part of the video and take brief notes on the answers to the following questions. Then compare your notes with those of another student.

14:35–
17:24

1. What two complaints did the cab drivers make in the taxi court?

   _____

2. What three languages does the Haitian driver, Pierre Jacquet Reynould, speak?

   _____

3. How much does the cab driver's training course cost? How long is the course?

   _____

4. Which streets in New York City go east? Which go west?

   _____

5. Why is the Waverly and Waverly intersection in Manhattan unusual?

   _____

6. Why do immigrants become cab drivers?

   _____

MAKING TRUE SENTENCES

Watch the last part of the video. Then use the chart to make five true
sentences. Write the sentences below. The first one has been done for you.

One of the commentators has . . .	1. lived in New York for 15 years.
	2. taken about a thousand cabs.
Neither commentator has . . .	3. had a bad experience in a cab.
	4. corresponded with a cab driver.
	5. met a philosopher cab driver.

1. *One of the commentators has lived in New York for 15 years.*

2. _____

3. _____

4. _____

5. _____

AFTER YOU WATCH

LANGUAGE POINT: GERUNDS AND INFINITIVES

The video contains a number of examples of *gerunds* and *infinitives*. Study
these sentences:

Drivers prepare for rude passenger by *playing* roles. (gerund)

Some taxi drivers refuse *to go* to certain areas. (infinitive)

Complete each of the following sentences with the *gerund* (verb + <u>ing</u>) or
infinitive (<u>to</u> + verb) of the verb in parentheses.

1. Taxicab passengers in New York can file a complaint that can force a
   driver (go) __To go__ to a taxi court.

2. Passengers complain about taxi drivers not (pick) __Picking__
   them up.

3. One passenger said, "I'm tired of (get) __getting__ refused."

4. Another one said, "He refused (let) _to let._ us out of the cab."

5. The passenger asked the driver (make) _to make_ . a left turn.

6. An old American joke goes like this: " How do you get to Carnegie Hall? By (practice) _practicing_ ."

VOCABULARY CHECK: COLLOQUIAL EXPRESSIONS

The following excerpts are from the video. What do the *italicized* words mean? Circle the answer that is closest in meaning.

1. You've *made it to* Kennedy Airport . . .
   a. gotten married at
   b. successfully arrived at
   c. succeeded at
   d. built it at

2. These are tough native New Yorkers *who know all the tricks.*
   a. understand magic
   b. have information about all the traffic lights
   c. are experts at playing cards
   d. know every way to cheat or mislead people

3. They'll cheat you on the fare, maybe *drop you off* at some hellhole miles away from your hotel.
   a. allow you to get out of the taxi
   b. push you out of the taxi
   c. lower your fare
   d. make you fall asleep

4. When cab drivers *live up to* the vicious (bad or wicked) stereotype, we customers can file a complaint.
   a. have apartments like
   b. enjoy
   c. want to be like
   d. act like

5. Tyrone Rice says this driver stopped, *looked* Rice *over,* and then drove on.
   a. searched for
   b. refused to notice
   c. examined quickly
   d. took care of

6. I think it's because they're scared a driver's going to rob them or *whatever.*
   a. something like that
   b. anything that takes forever
   c. nothing you want to do
   d. everything you want to do

7. Do some passengers *have an attitude?*
   a. look surprised
   b. look bored
   c. act in a friendly way
   d. act in an unfriendly way

8. Watching these students beginning a new life, eager to *make it* in America . . .
   a. build it
   b. get married
   c. succeed
   d. arrive

DISCUSSION

Work in groups. Discuss your answers to the following questions.

1. What are the arguments for and against some cab drivers' behavior?

2. What experiences have you had with cab drivers? Describe some good experiences.

3. Compare the ways cabs operate in New York City with the way cabs operate in your country.

4. The news report says that some immigrants in New York become taxi drivers. What are some typical jobs that new immigrants do in your country? What advice would you give to a new immigrant to help him or her get started in your country?

ROLE PLAY

Work in pairs. One student will pay the role of a taxi driver. The other will play the role of a passenger. Read the role descriptions and then choose one of the situations listed. Don't tell your partner which situation you chose. Act out the scene. Then change roles and do the role play again.

ROLE DESCRIPTION: **Taxi Drivers**
1. It's very late at night. You are worried about robbery.
2. You have just decided to stop work and go home for the day.
3. It's a beautiful, sunny day. You feel happy and relaxed.
4. The traffic is terrible. You take a longer route to avoid it.
5. You help the passenger with his or her baggage.

ROLE DESCRIPTION: **Passengers**
1. You have just arrived in the city after a very long plane trip. You are tired and look very untidy.
2. You are seriously ill. You need to get to a hospital fast.
3. You are late for a business meeting downtown.
4. You think the taxi driver has overcharged you.
5. You are pleased with the service and give the driver a big tip.

READING

Read the article, *Taking a Taxi in the United States*. Then decide if the complaints that follow the article are *fair* or *unfair* according to the information in the reading. Write **F** (fair) or **U** (unfair).

TAKING A TAXI IN THE UNITED STATES

I've taken cabs in cities from New York to San Francisco, but I've never met an "American" cab driver. The drivers have been from Cuba, Jamaica, Iran, Russia, Greece, and Hong Kong — but never, in my experience, 'born in the U.S.A.'

If you're taking a cab in the United States, it helps to know the rules. That way you will avoid unnecessary confrontation when the driver is in the right and you're in the wrong. Taxis are metered all over the country, but in cities like New York and Chicago, the meter will show a fare of at least $1.00 before the cab starts moving. In some cities, such as Washington, D.C., taxis operate on a distance zone system. In some cities it is legal to share a cab with strangers. If so, you should pay the full price even if you are sharing. You need to check the rules of the city you are in.

Getting a taxi

You can hail a cab on the street or find one at a taxi stand, a special parking area reserved for taxis (In some cities these areas may be called "cabstands" or "hack stands.") You can also telephone for a cab. The local telephone book will list the numbers.

Your rights

As in other countries, U.S. taxi drivers must stop if you hail them, unless they are showing an off-duty sign. They must drive anywhere you ask them to go within the city limits, and they can't ask your destination before you get in and then refuse to take you there. They must charge what the meter says, except for trunks, bridge or tunnel tolls, and special late night fees. In some cases the driver-passenger negotiation can be very personal. A cab driver may do you a favor or ask you to do one for him.

Baggage

Don't be annoyed if a driver doesn't get out of the cab to help you with your baggage. In areas where there is heavy traffic, it may be illegal — for safety reasons — for drivers to get out of their cabs to open doors.

SOME COMPLAINTS ABOUT TAXI DRIVERS:

1. __Y__ I shared a cab with a stranger. The driver charged each of us the full fare.

2. __F__ I told the driver my destination. He didn't want to go there.

3. __X__ My house is on the other side of the toll bridge over the river. The driver charged me for the toll.

4. _____ I hailed a cab, but the driver didn't stop.

5. _____ I live downtown. I had five suitcases and took a cab home. The driver didn't get out and help me when we arrived there.

6. _____ It cost a dollar just to get in and sit down!

WRITING

Complete one of the following activities.

1. You are an unhappy passenger. You think a cab driver overcharged you by $20. Write a letter of complaint to the cab company. Describe the details of your journey, how much you paid the driver, how much you think the fare really was, and ask for some money back. Give the driver's hack number.

2. You are a taxi driver. You think the program *Those Terrible Taxis!* was unfair. Write a letter to ABC News, telling them what your job is like and what problems you encounter daily.

3. A friend is coming to visit you from another country or city. Write and tell your friend to get a cab from the airport or station to your house. Give your friend advice about what kind of cab to get, how much to pay, and what tip to give.

Segment 4

Maya Angelou, Inaugural Poetess

From: *World News Tonight, 1/22/93*
Begin: 18:21
Length: 5:05

BEFORE YOU WATCH

TALKING POINTS

Work in groups. Discuss your answers to the following questions.

1. What is an "inauguration"? What is the purpose of an inauguration? Where do inaugurations usually take place?

2. Have you ever attended an inauguration or seen one on television? If so, describe it. Whose inauguration was it? Who spoke at the inauguration? What did the speakers talk about?

3. Why do you think Maya Angelou is described as an inaugural poetess?

PREDICTING

Based on the title of the video segment, *Maya Angelou, Inaugural Poetess*, what do you think you will see and hear on the video? Write down five items under each of the headings below. Then compare your answers with those of another student.

<table>
<tr><td align="center">SIGHTS
(things you expect to see)</td><td align="center">WORDS
(words you expect to hear)</td></tr>
<tr><td>1. _____</td><td>_____</td></tr>
<tr><td>2. _____</td><td>_____</td></tr>
<tr><td>3. _____</td><td>_____</td></tr>
<tr><td>4. _____</td><td>_____</td></tr>
<tr><td>5. _____</td><td>_____</td></tr>
</table>

KEY WORDS

The *italicized* words in the sentences below will help you understand the video. Study the sentences. Then write your own definition of each word.

1. Her words had a great *influence* upon her listeners.

   influence: _____

2. Because of television, a *vast* audience of people around the world heard her speech.

   vast: _____

3. The reporter decided to *paraphrase* the original words of the writer.

   paraphrase: _____

4. Some people have more power and *privilege* than others.

   privilege: _____

5. She founded an organization to help women who have been *raped*.

   raped: _____

6. Until the middle of the twentieth century, people in the southern part of the United States were racially *segregated*.

   segregated: _____

7. The actor will *render* a speech from Shakespeare's *Hamlet*.

   render: _____

8. He had the *grace* to smile and try to comfort her.

   grace: _____

WHILE YOU WATCH

18:30–
23:18

GETTING THE MAIN IDEA

Watch the news report and listen for the answers to the following questions. Take brief notes on the answers. Then compare your answers with those of another student.

What has Maya Angelou done? **Where**?
Why is this important?

What?	
Where?	
Why?	

CHECKING YOUR PREDICTIONS

Look at the lists you made in the PREDICTING exercise on page 31. Watch the video and check (✔) the items that you actually see and hear.

18:30–
23:18

WHAT'S MISSING?

Listen to the Peter Jennings's introduction to the news report. Fill in the missing words.

18:37–
18:54

Peter Jennings: Finally, this evening, our Person of the Week, by way of
(1) _____ really, because it's (2) _____ that you
(3) _____ her this week. The day before yesterday, this
woman was given an (4) _____ opportunity to have an
(5) _____ on a (6) _____ audience of people. And to
(7) _____ her message then, she certainly (8) _____
the moment.

LISTENING FOR DETAILS

Watch the video again. Circle the correct answers.

19:07–
21:51

1. Who invited Maya Angelou to speak at his presidential inauguration?
   a. Ronald Reagan.
   b. George Bush.
   c. Bill Clinton.

2. How long has she sung, danced, acted, taught, written, and recited?
   a. 14 years.
   b. 32 years.
   c. 40 years.

3. Where did she grow up?
   a. In Washington, D.C.
   b. In Stamps, Arkansas.
   c. In Los Angeles, California.

4. Who did she live with in the back of a store?
   a. Her grandmother and her uncle.
   b. Her father and her grandmother.
   c. Her mother.

5. What did Maya Angelou refuse to do for 5 and a half years?
   a. Dance.
   b. Speak.
   c. Write.

6. When she decided to use her voice again, what did she recite in the Seamee Church?
   a. A poem by Langston Hughes.
   b. A speech from William Shakespeare's *The Merchant of Venice*.
   c. A speech she had written herself.

19:15–
22:54

MAKING INFERENCES

Watch the video. Check (✔) the sentences that are *probably* true about Maya Angelou.

1. __F__ Maya Angelou has spoken at many presidential inaugurations.
2. __F__ She still lives near Stamps, Arkansas.
3. __✓__ She experienced a lot of sadness as a child.
4. __F__ She believes Americans should be proud of their history.
5. __✓__ She thinks Americans must accept their history.
6. __✓__ She feels all people in America must accept one another.
7. __F__ She thinks Americans should stop trying to change their country.
8. __✓__ She is hopeful about the future of America.

21:56–
23:13

MAKING TRUE SENTENCES

Watch the last part of the video. Then use the chart below to make four true sentences. Write the sentences below.

1. Maya Angelou . . .	were heard by millions of people at once.
2. American poets . . .	are often heard by 20,000 people.
3. Russian poets . . .	rarely perform before thousands of people.
4. Maya Angelou's words . . .	delivered a speech from the steps of the U.S. Capitol.

1. _____

2. _____

3. _____

4. _____

LANGUAGE POINT: PASSIVE PAST TENSE

On the video, Peter Jennings uses the *passive past tense* (*was* or *were* + past participle) when he says, "Maya *was raised* by her grandmother and uncle."

We use passive past tense to emphasize what happened to someone. We use a "*by* phrase" in passive sentences when it is important to know who performed an action.

Change the sentences below to the past passive. Include the "*by* phrase" if necessary. The first one has been done for you.

1. Someone gave Maya Angelou an opportunity to talk to millions of people.

   Maya Angelou was given an opportunity to talk to millions of people.

2. President Clinton engaged her to speak at his inauguration.

   _____

   _____

3. For the first time in 32 years, someone asked a poet to speak at a presidential inauguration.

   _____

   _____

4. The poet recited her speech from the steps of the Capitol.

   _____

   _____

5. Millions of people all over the world heard her words.

   _____

   _____

COLLOQUIAL EXPRESSIONS

The excerpts below are from the video. What do the *italicized* expressions mean? Circle the answer that is closest in meaning.

1. It was going to *knock them off those pews*.
   a. amaze them
   b. make them worry
   c. sadden them
   d. make them fall to the floor

2. She certainly *seized the moment.*
   a. wasted the opportunity
   (b.) made good use of the opportunity
   c. took a long time
   d. kept her eyes on the clock

3. We have no chance of *building a tomorrow* for our children.
   a. believing in the future
   b. predicting the future
   c. understanding the future
   (d.) creating a future

VOCABULARY CHECK

The *italicized* words are used on the video. Cross out the word or phrase in each row that does not have a similar meaning to the word in *italics*.

1. *recited*   performed orally   spoken   ~~silenced~~
2. *humiliated*   ~~honored~~   shamed   disgraced
3. *neglected*   ignored   ~~desired~~   abandoned
4. *whence*   ~~the time when~~   the place which   where
5. *urged*   advised   recommended   ~~discouraged~~

CATEGORIZING WORDS

On the video, Maya Angelou uses the words below to refer to some of the many different groups of people that make up American society. In which category does each word belong? Check (✔) the most appropriate box.

	Ethnic Group	Religion	Profession	Sexual Orientation	Economic Situation
1. Catholic	❏	☒	❏	❏	❏
2. Muslim	❏	☒	❏	❏	❏
3. French	☒	❏	❏	❏	❏
4. Greek	☒	❏	❏	❏	❏
5. Irish	☒	❏	❏	❏	❏
6. rabbi	❏	❏	☒	❏	❏
7. priest	❏	❏	☒	❏	❏
8. sheik (?)	❏	❏	☒	❏	❏
9. gay (?)	❏	❏	❏	☒	❏
10. straight (?)	❏	❏	❏	☒	❏
11. preacher (?)	❏	❏	☒	❏	❏

12. privileged	❏	❏	❏	❏	☒
13. homeless	❏	❏	❏	❏	☒
14. teacher	❏	❏	☒	❏	❏

DICTIONARY DEFINITIONS

The words below are used on the video. Each word has more than one definition. Read the definitions and the sentences. Then match the correct definition with the sentence.

EXAMPLE: *engage*:   a. to name or chose
          b. to interest or get the attention of

__b__ Maya Angelou's words *engaged* a huge audience.

__a__ President Clinton *engaged* Maya Angelou to speak at his inauguration.

1. *suspend*:   a. to hang from a support from above
          b. to delay or stop from being active for a period of time

__b__ When Maya Angelou reads poetry, she tries to *suspend* herself and get into the content of the poem.

__a__ Three large lamps are *suspended* from the classroom ceiling.

2. *posture*:   a. attitude or way of looking at something
          b. way of holding the body

__a__ The government is taking a more positive *posture* toward the peace plan.

__b__ Good *posture* is important for a dancer.

3. *piercing*:   a. sharp or intense
          b. cutting through or into (something)

__a__ Maya Angelou told the audience, "You have a *piercing* need for this bright new morning dawning for you."

__b__ He was *piercing* the rubber ball with a knife.

4. *wrenching*:   a. pulling or twisting
          b. sorrowful

__b__ In Maya Angelou's speech, she mentioned the *wrenching* pain of history.

__a__ She was *wrenching* the button off the coat.

5. *pulse*:   a. thrill of life or emotion
                b. regular beating of the heart, as it pumps blood through the body

<u>A</u>   Maya Angelou said, "Here, on the *pulse* of this new day, you may have the grace to look into your sister's eyes and into your brother's face."

<u>b</u>   The nurse felt the patient's *pulse*.

DISCUSSION

Work in groups. Discuss your answers to the following questions.

1. When presidents choose a figure to make an inaugural speech, they choose someone who represents ideas and principles they believe in. Why do you think President Clinton chose Maya Angelou?

2. Peter Jennings says that in Russia, 20,000 people will show up to hear a poet. How important is poetry in your culture? In your opinion, who is the most important poet? How influential is he or she?

3. Maya Angelou is a famous American poet. What other American writers have you heard of? Have you read any of their works? What other American writers do you like? Why?

ROLE PLAY

Work in pairs. One student will play the role of the interviewer. The other will play the role of the famous person. Read the situation and role descriptions that follow and decide who will play each role. After a ten-minute preparation, begin the interview.

THE SITUATION: **A TV Interview**

A TV program called "ABC Interviews" has invited a famous person to talk about his or her background, education, and career.

ROLE DESCRIPTION: **Interviewer**

You are an interviewer for "ABC Interviews." After your partner has told you which famous person he or she is, make notes about what you know about the person. If necessary, ask other students what they know. Be prepared to ask questions about the person's date and place of birth, family background, home life, education, how the person discovered his or her talent, how he or she became famous, and so forth.

You are a famous person. Be prepared to answer questions about your date and place of birth, family background, home life, education, talent, and how you became famous.

READING

Read the article below to find out about a person that inspired Maya Angelou. Then answer the questions that follow.

MAYA ANGELOU REMEMBERS MISS KIRWIN

Maya Angelou was in town recently. I heard her on the local radio station. Her voice was deep and like gravel. She spoke slowly, but her mind was sharp and full of wit. If you know her background and where she came from, you can understand why she is such an inspiration. In her autobiography, *I Know Why the Caged Bird Sings,* Maya Angelou wrote about a woman who served as an inspiration to her during her teenage years.

In the early 1940s, when Maya Angelou was thirteen, she moved from the small town of Stamps, Arkansas, to San Francisco, California, a city which she came to love and where she became free of the fears that had characterized so much of her life in rural Arkansas. Shortly after her arrival in the city, she was enrolled in George Washington High School, which she describes as "the first real school" she attended.

The high school was sixty blocks from the San Francisco neighborhood in which Maya Angelou lived, and she was one of only three black students in the school. At first she was disappointed to find that — in contrast to her experience at the schools she had previously attended — she was not the smartest or even close to being the smartest student. The white students had better vocabularies and were far less fearful in the classroom. They never hesitated to respond to the teacher's questions — even when they were wrong. She, on the other hand, never volunteered unless she was absolutely certain her answer was correct.

Her time at George Washington High School wasn't wasted, however. There she was inspired by one of her teachers, Miss Kirwin. According to Maya Angelou, Miss Kirwin was "in love with information" and loved teaching not because of the students, but because she felt they represented places where information could be stored and later passed on to others.

"Miss Kirwin," said Maya Angelou, "had been teaching in the San Francisco city school system for more than twenty years. She was a tall, gray-haired, red-faced woman who taught civics and current affairs. Maybe because of her enthusiasm for up-to-date information, Miss Kirwin never used textbooks, even though the students had them. She based her lessons on newspaper and magazine articles rather than books. The articles she selected were about subjects like the mining industry in the Carolinas and other contemporary issues, rather than the topics in the students' traditional schoolbooks." As a result, Maya Angelou and all of Miss Kirwin's other students became excited about reading. Within a few weeks after joining Miss Kirwin's class, Maya Angelou was regularly reading the local newspapers, magazines like *Time* and *Life*, and just about everything else that was available to her.

Another reason that Maya Angelou admired Miss Kirwin was that — unlike most adults — Miss Kirwin treated her teenage students with respect. She addressed them as "ladies and gentlemen," rather than calling them "class" or "students." And she was fair. She had no favorite students, no "teacher's pets." No one in her class received special treatment. If Maya Angelou or any other student had the right answer to a question, Miss Kirwin never said anything more than the word "correct."

1. According to Maya Angelou, in what two ways were the white kids at George Washington High School different from her?

   _____

   _____

2. What are three things that Maya Angelou liked about Miss Kirwin?

   _____

   _____

3. What was Miss Kirwin's attitude regarding textbooks? How do you know? Do you agree with her attitude? Why or why not?

   _____

   _____

4. What kinds of things did the students in Miss Kirwin's class read?

   _____

   _____

WRITING

Complete one of the following activities.

1. What person would you invite to open a new school or college or to present a prize? Write a letter of invitation to that person. Explain what the event is, where and when it will be held, and why you would like that person to come.

2. What would you say if you had the chance to speak to the American nation on national TV or radio? Write a 150–200 word speech to the people of the United States.

Segment 5
Paul Simon

From: *World News Tonight,* 10/22/93
Begin: 23:29
Length: 5:11

BEFORE YOU WATCH

TALKING POINTS

Work in groups. Discuss your answers to the following questions.

1. What kind of music do you like? classical? pop? folk? jazz? some other kind?

2. Do you have a favorite song? If so, what is it? What is the song about?

3. Paul Simon is a famous American singer and compŏser. What do you know about him? Make a list.

4. Have you ever heard any of Paul Simon's music? If so, do you like it? Why or why not?

PREDICTING

The video is about the career of Paul Simon, a famous American singer and songwriter. What are some names that you expect to hear on the video? Complete the following chart with your predictions.

Name of a Song	Sounds of Silence
Name of a Musician (other than Paul Simon)	Art Garfunkel
Name of a Country (other than the U.S.A.)	South Africa

KEY WORDS

The *italicized* words in the sentences below will help you understand the video. Study the sentences. Then match the words with the meanings.

1. His fame has *endured* throughout the years.
2. She becomes *nostalgic* when she hears her favorite old song.
3. A recording company just *released* a new album of his songs.
4. He is performing in a *retrospective* concert of his music.
5. The *lyrics* go well with the music.
6. By the late 1960s, many Americans were in *rebellion* against the war in Vietnam.
7. The song *signified* the country's loss of innocence.
8. Many countries joined the economic *boycott* against South Africa.
9. The music is a *blend* of African and Latin American influences.
10. That singer is popular and has always been a big *draw* at concerts.

1. __d__ *endured*
2. __g__ *nostalgic*
3. __e__ *released*
4. __i__ *retrospective*
5. __c__ *lyrics*
6. __h__ *rebellion*
7. __a__ *signified*
8. __j__ *boycott*
9. _____ *blend*
10. _____ *draw* (n)

a. meant or symbolized
b. a person or thing that attracts an audience
c. the words of a song
d. continued for a long time
e. permitted to be sold
f. a mixture
g. full of good memories of things in the past
h. resistance or strong protest
i. looking on a person's past artistic work
j. a joint refusal to do business with a country

WHILE YOU WATCH

23:36–
28:32

GETTING THE MAIN IDEA

Watch the news report and listen for the answers to the following questions. Take brief notes on the answers. Then compare your answers with those of another student.

> **Who** is Paul Simon and **what** made him famous (popular)?
>
> **When** did Paul Simon have his first hit?

Why is his music important?

How has his music changed over the years?

Who?	
What?	
When?	
Why?	
How?	

CHECKING YOUR PREDICTIONS

Look at the chart you completed in the PREDICTING exercise on page 41. Watch the video and check (✔) the names that you actually hear.

23:36–28:32

WHAT'S MISSING?

Listen to Peter Jennings's introduction to the news report. Fill in the missing words.

23:44–24:06

Peter Jennings: Finally, this evening, our Person of the Week —
someone very (1) _____ . A man who has certainly
(2) _____ and who manages after, lo, these many years
to remind more than one (3) _____ that talent is a
gift and (4) _____ that gift has made a great deal of
(5) _____ to a great many people. We choose him this
week because we're at that (6) _____ to be (7) _____
and because he keeps moving his (8) _____ forward.

* * *

Paul Simon, the (9) _____ singer who turned 52 last week,
has no intention of slip-sliding away to anywhere. He has just
released the (10) _____ works of 30 years and this week he
is performing in a sold-out, 21-show retrospective concert, *Back
Together Again*, with his former partner, Art Garfunkel.

NOTETAKING

Watch the video and fill in the chart with the correct information.

24:08–
26:07

Paul Simon's age when he became interested in making records and writing songs	13
Paul Simon's age at the time this news report was broadcast	52
Number of years covered in Paul Simon's collected works	30
Number of shows in the *Back Together Again* concert	21
Year in which Paul Simon wrote the music and lyrics of *Mrs. Robinson*	1967
Number of copies sold of *A Bridge Over Troubled Water*	10'000.000.

PUTTING EVENTS IN ORDER

24:08–
28:03

Read the sentences below which describe the events in Paul Simon's career. Then watch the video and put the events in the order in which they actually happened. Number them from 1 to 10. The first and last events have been numbered for you. To complete the exercise, you may need to watch the video several times.

__4__ He recorded "Bridge Over Troubled Water" with Art Garfunkel.

__5__ He and Garfunkel performed in New York's Central Park.

__2__ He recorded "The Sounds of Silence" with Art Garfunkel.

__10__ He and Garfunkel performed in the *Back Together Again* concert.

__3__ He wrote the music and lyrics for *The Graduate*.

__7__ He began to incorporate the music and influences of other cultures in his work.

__9__ He released the recording of his collective works.

__6__ He and Garfunkel broke up.

__1__ Paul Simon first became interested in making records and writing songs.

__8__ He made the *Graceland* album with Ladysmith Black Mambazo.

LISTENING FOR DETAILS

Watch the video. Circle the correct answers.

24:52–26:19

1. According to Peter Jennings and Jon Pareles, what special quality do Paul Simon's lyrics have?
   a. Timelessness.
   b. Timeliness.
   c. Innocence.

2. Who was Paul Simon's childhood friend in New York?
   a. Dustin Hoffman.
   b. Mrs. Robinson.
   c. Art Garfunkel.

3. What Simon and Garfunkel song was a big hit in 1965?
   a. "The Sounds of Silence"
   b. "Mrs. Robinson"
   c. "Bridge Over Troubled Water"

4. What did the song "Mrs. Robinson" signify?
   a. Paul Simon's graduation from high school.
   b. The country's support of the war.
   c. The country's loss of innocence.

5. Why did Simon and Garfunkel break up?
   a. They didn't like each other.
   b. Simon's musical ideas were changing.
   c. They were living in different places.

MAKING INFERENCES

Watch the video and check (✔) the sentences that are probably true.

26:25–28:18

1. _____ Ladysmith Black Mambazo is a South African group.

2. _____ Before they recorded the *Graceland* album with Paul Simon, Ladysmith Black Mambazo was already internationally famous.

3. _____ The members of Ladysmith Black Mambazo thought that Paul Simon exploited them.

4. _____ People enjoy watching Paul Simon and Art Garfunkel perform.

5. _____ Paul Simon has had a greater influence on American music than Art Garfunkel has.

6. _____ Paul Simon is as concerned with his professional career as he is with his music.

LANGUAGE POINT: A GREAT DEAL OF, A GREAT MANY

On the video, Peter Jennings says that Paul Simon's music "has made *a great deal of* difference to *a great many people*." We use the quantifier *a great deal of* with uncountable nouns. We use *a great many* with countable plural nouns. Complete each sentence with either *a great deal of* or *a great many*, whichever is appropriate.

1. Since the age of 13, Paul Simon has had _____ interest in making records and writing music.

2. He and Art Garfunkel were childhood friends, and they worked together for _____ years.

3. Since the 1970s, Paul Simon has worked with _____ other musicians.

4. His music has incorporated _____ influences of other cultures.

5. The *Graceland* album introduced the music of Ladysmith Black Mambazo to _____ people outside South Africa.

6. Paul Simon has had _____ success in his 30-year career.

Home work

VOCABULARY CHECK: COLLOQUIAL EXPRESSIONS

The following excerpts are from the video. What do the *italicized* expressions mean? Circle the correct answer.

1. And he can do that, and he can *make it stick in your head*.
   - a. make you do something silly
   - b. make you forget it
   - c. make you remember it
   - d. make you sing it

2. So we *were just in very different places*, musically.
   - a. stayed in different towns
   - b. came from different traditions
   - c. lived in different countries
   - d. had very different ideas

3. They *broke up* a year later.
   - a. became lucky
   - b. separated
   - c. became depressed
   - d. experienced failure

4. It was in the '70s that Paul Simon began to incorporate the music and influences of other cultures that would *mold his social message*.
   - a. sing his social message
   - b. write about his social message
   - c. criticize his social message
   - d. influence his social message

5. He *took a lot of heat* for going to South Africa.
   a. was criticized
   b. got hot
   c. became popular
   d. carried a heater

6. It *made for* a powerful international blend, with African and American influence.
   a. avoided
   b. weakened
   c. resulted in
   d. stole

7. But it is Paul Simon who's always made such a difference to American music, who has always *gone on to greater heights*.
   a. continued to grow taller
   b. continued to become more successful
   c. sung in a higher voice
   d. traveled in more mountainous areas

8. Pretty fast to be *going through* his history, but there you are.
   a. beginning
   b. ending
   c. reviewing
   d. writing

FINDING THE OPPOSITES ~~Have work~~

The excerpts below are from the video. Look in the box and find the word or phrase that is the opposite of each *italicized* word. The first one has been done for you.

failure	separate	excluding	slightly	bored
weak	union	unknown	using fairly	abundance

1. ___unknown___ Finally, this evening, our Person of the Week — someone very *familiar*.

2. _____ I became *fascinated* with making records.

3. _____ "The Sounds of Silence" was a huge *hit* for them in 1965.

4. _____ Simon wrote the music and lyrics for *The Graduate* in 1967, *including* the song "Mrs. Robinson."

5. _____ For many, the song signified the country's loss of innocence and the *dearth* of heroes for a generation in rebellion against an unpopular war.

6. _____ I probably had begun that *separation* during the making of "Bridge Over Troubled Water."

7. _____ It was in the '70s that Simon began to *incorporate* the music and other influences of other cultures.

8. _____ He was accused of breaking the economic boycott and *exploiting* South African black performers.

9. _____ And *Graceland* was an *enormously* successful album.

10. _____ It made for a *powerful* international blend, with African and American influence.

DISCUSSION

Work in groups. Discuss your answers to the following questions.

1. In addition to Paul Simon, what other American singers are you familiar with? What are some of their songs? Which of their songs do you like the best?

2. Is American popular music widely heard in your culture? Which American performers are most often heard on radio or TV in your country?

3. For many Americans, the song "Mrs. Robinson" had great cultural and political significance. Think about songs produced by your own society or culture. Which songs have been important and why?

4. For 30 years Paul Simon has been one of the most popular songwriters and singers in the United States. What songwriters or singers in your culture have had the most enduring popularity? Why do you think these people have experienced such great success?

ROLE PLAY

Work in pairs. One student will play the role of the interviewer. The other will play the role of Paul Simon. Read the situation and the role descriptions below and decide who will play each role. After a ten-minute preparation, begin the interview.

SITUATION: **A Radio Interview**

A radio program called "Music Matters" has invited Paul Simon to talk about his career as a singer and songwriter.

ROLE DESCRIPTION: **Interviewer**

You are the interviewer for "Music Matters." Prepare a list of questions to ask Paul Simon about his career as a singer and songwriter.

ROLE DESCRIPTION: **Paul Simon**

You are Paul Simon. Be prepared to answer questions about your career as a singer and songwriter.

READING

Read the article below to find out about the origins of rock music. Then use the information in the article to do the tasks that follow.

THE STORY OF ROCK

Paul Simon's influences include South African harmonies and Latin American rhythms. But where did Elvis Presley, the Rolling Stones, and Bruce Springsteen get their beat?

Popular music in the United States developed from two sets of influences. First was the traditional music of the Africans who were brought to America as slaves to work on the plantations. They were forbidden to use their traditional musical instruments, so they adapted their African music and created rhythmical work songs. When the slaves later converted to Christianity, they developed gospel music, a powerful and beautiful style of religious singing based on African musical patterns. The second great influence on American popular music was European. Immigrants to the United States carried their own folk music and musical instruments with them across the Atlantic.

In the 19th and 20th centuries these two great musical traditions came together — despite segregation — through jazz and other popular musical styles. Later, the black work songs of the rural South spread to the cities of the North and developed into rhythm and blues. This was the basis of what we now call "rock 'n' roll," the energetic music that became widely popular with American teenagers in the 1950s. Today we associate rock music ewith black and white musicians qually, but its earlier form, rock 'n' roll, was first popularized by white singers such as Elvis Presley and white groups such as Bill Haley and the Comets. These musicians took the rhythm and blues songs, which had been originally performed by black musicians such as Chuck Berry, and made them popular with young Americans. The great blues singer Muddy Waters once said, "Rhythm and blues had a baby, and they called it rock 'n' roll."

A short time afterward, gospel music was also "having a baby." Black singers such as Little Richard, James Brown, and Aretha Franklin adapted the style, but not the religious content, of gospel music to popular music, and they called the new baby "soul music." One of the most famous examples of soul music is Berry Gordy's Motown Sound, based in Detroit, America's motor city.

Even today, black music provides the basis of popular music in the United States, including reggae from Jamaica and rap from America's inner cities. When Paul Simon made South African musicians popular worldwide through his *Graceland* album, he was doing what others had done before him — going back to black musical roots.

1. Which musical style is associated with each musician? Check (✔) the appropriate columns.

	Blues	Soul	Rhythm & Blues	Rock 'n' Roll
Muddy Waters				
Bill Haley				
Elvis Presley				✗
James Brown				
Aretha Franklin			✗	
Chuck Berry			✗	

2. Put these musical styles in their historical order. Number them from 1 to 7. The first one has been done for you.

_____ rock 'n' roll   _____ rap

__1__ work songs   _____ rhythm and blues

_____ jazz   _____ soul music

_____ gospel music

3. What does Paul Simon's *Graceland* album have in common with earlier forms of popular music in the United States?

_____

WRITING

Complete one of the following activities.

1. You are a book publisher and are soon to publish a biography of Paul Simon. You haven't yet written the text to go on the back cover. Write a short text (150–200 words) that you think will interest people and make them want to buy the book.

2. Write a letter to the producer of the TV news *World News Tonight,* giving your opinion of Peter Jennings's news report on Paul Simon.

Segment 6
Poetry in America

From: *ABC News Nightline*, 6/18/92
Begin: 28:43
Length: 8:52

BEFORE YOU WATCH

TALKING POINTS

Work in groups. Discuss your answers to the following questions.

1. When was the last time you read or listened to a poem? What was its title? Who wrote it? What was it about?

2. Did you read or learn about poetry at school? If so, did you enjoy it? Explain your answer.

3. Look at the words below. Which ones best describe your view of poetry?

    easy   literary   serious   fun   a cheap night out

    difficult   popular   necessary   expensive   useless

PREDICTING

Based on the title of the video, *Poetry in America*, predict the kinds of information you think will be included on the video.

1. _____

2. _____

3. _____

4. _____

5. _____

KEY WORDS

The *italicized* words in the sentences below will help you understand the video. Study the sentences. Then match the words with the meanings.

1. She wrote a *polemical* book about the need to reform the educational system.
2. The words "hear" and "dear" *rhyme* with "near."
3. The pianist forgot his music, so everything he played was *improvised*.
4. I like the music of this song, but I don't like the *lyrics*.
5. She enjoys listening to *oral* poetry more than reading poetry in books.
6. Shakespeare's fame as a poet is *enduring*.
7. I have an *anthology* of seventeenth-century English poetry.
8. He says that better *marketing* will result in higher sales.
9. They're opening a new bookstore in the *mall*.
10. Every person who is *literate* should read this book.

1. _h_ *polemical*
2. _b_ *rhyme*
3. _e_ *improvised*
4. _d_ *lyrics*
5. _A_ *oral*
6. _i_ *enduring*
7. _F_ *anthology*
8. _J_ *marketing*
9. _G_ *mall*
10. _A_ *literate*

a. able to read and write
b. to end with the same sound
c. spoken, not written
d. the words of a song
e. made up while being performed
f. a collection of writings by different authors published together in one book
g. area with rows of stores, closed to traffic
h. strongly arguing for or against an opinion
i. permanent or long lasting
j. the different things that are done to advertise and sell a product

---

WHILE YOU WATCH

GETTING THE MAIN IDEA

Watch the news report and listen for the answers to the following questions. Take brief notes on the answers. Then compare your answers with those of another student.

29:31–
37:28

Who is doing **what**, **where**?
Why and **how** are they doing this?

Who?	
What?	
Where?	
Why?	
How?	

CHECKING YOUR PREDICTIONS

Look at the lists you made in the PREDICTING exercise on page 51. Watch the video and check (✔) the items that you actually see and hear.

29:31– 37:28

WHAT'S MISSING?

Listen to Ted Koppel's introduction to the news report. Fill in the missing words.

29:51– 33:32

Ted Koppel: When I was a (1) _____ , growing up in England, parents – not just mine, but almost all parents – placed enormous stock in the (2) _____–_____ power of cod liver oil. Despite the fact that I was repeatedly told how (3) _____ it was for me, I learned to loathe cod liver oil. Unfortunately, some parents and many teachers dispense (4) _____ the same way. We would like, if humanly possible, to undo some of that (5) _____ tonight. Indeed, perhaps a (6) _____ is in order. Poetry has the power to arouse and inflame, to evoke the most private of emotions. It can be polemical or funny. It can rhyme, but it doesn't have to, and there is some (7) _____ that you may (8) _____ it.

CHECKING WHAT YOU HEAR

30:48– 32:48

Listen to the next part of the news report. What are the features of the poetry readings at the Nuyorican Poets' Cafe? Check (✔) the points that Bob Holman, Dave Marash, and Miguel Algarin mention.

1. ☒ words you can dance to
2. ☒ low-cost weekend dates
3. ☒ fun and popular
4. ☒ young and alive

5. ❑ written poetry
6. ☒ oral poetry
7. ☒ improvised poetry
8. ❑ traditional poetry

LISTENING FOR DETAILS

32:25– 33:20

Watch the video. Circle the correct answers.

1. According to Joseph Brodsky, the Poet Laureate, what kind of poetry isn't reaching enough people?
   a. Pop lyrics.
   b. Improvised poetry.
   c. Poetry in print.

2. How does Brodsky think we can get more people to read poetry?
   a. By printing more poetry.
   b. By putting poetry before more people.
   c. Both a and b.

3. What would Brodsky like put in the drawer of every motel room in the United States?
   a. An anthology of American poets.
   b. The Bible.
   c. *The National Enquirer.*

4. Which newspaper wrote Brodsky a letter offering to print American poetry?
   a. *The Globe.*
   b. *The National Enquirer.*
   c. *The Star.*

5. In which place would Brodsky like to see books of poems for sale?
   a. In hotel rooms.
   b. In supermarkets.
   c. In the Library of Congress.

6. Which American poet is mentioned by both Dave Marash and Wieseltier?
   a. Robert Frost.
   b. Edgar Allan Poe.
   c. Emily Dickinson.

TRUE OR FALSE?

Watch the video. Are the following statements *true* or *false*? Write **T** (true) or **F** (false). Make the false statements true by changing one or two words.

33:46–36:56

1. __F__ Jane Friedman thinks Brodsky's idea is a possible dream.
2. __T__ The great books in *Everyman's Library* cost $15 to $22 each.
3. __T__ Richard Wilbur thinks that books of poetry are too expensive.
4. __F__ Richard Wilbur and Mark Strand believe that mass marketing can create a big audience for poetry.
5. __T__ Mark Strand thinks that people have to be educated to feel that poetry is necessary.
6. __T__ The *Writer's Voice* program organizes poetry readings by published and unpublished writers.
7. __F__ Roy Blount, Jr., thinks that great writers have always written for small audiences.
8. __F__ Bob Holman thinks that the only important poetry is the kind that you need a college education to understand.

AFTER YOU WATCH

LANGUAGE POINT: GIVING AN OPINION

On the video, former Poet Laureate Richard Wilbur gives his opinion when he says, "I think that books of poetry are frighteningly priced at present." Here are five common ways to introduce an opinion:

   a. I (don't) think (that)
   b. I (don't) feel (that)
   c. I (don't) believe (that)
   d. In my view,
   e. In my opinion,

Answer each of the following questions by giving an opinion. Introduce your opinion with expression a, b, c, d, or e, as indicated.

Example: Jane Friedman thinks it's impossible to produce good books cheaply. What do you think? (c)

   I believe it is difficult but not impossible.

1. What do you think of the idea of selling books of poetry in supermarkets? (a)

_____

2. How do you feel about the idea that people have to be educated to feel that poetry is necessary? (b)

_____

3. According to Roy Blount, Jr., the greatest writers have always written for small audiences. What's your view? (d)

_____

4. Joseph Brodsky thinks everybody is a potential reader of poetry. What do you think? (e)

_____

5. Which do you think is worse — burning books or not reading them? (e)

_____

VOCABULARY CHECK

The following excerpts are from the video. What do the italicized words and expressions mean? Circle the answer that is closest in meaning.

Words *shimmy* and *slam* out of M.C. Bob Holman's mouth as he *launches* another set of improvised poetry at New York's Nuyorican Poets' Cafe.

1. *shimmy and slam*:
   a. come quickly and softly
   b. come quickly and loudly
   c. come slowly and loudly
   d. come slowly and softly

2. *launches*:
   a. starts
   b. interrupts
   c. forgets
   d. finishes

It's clear that this new game, *tongue-in-cheek* thing that we have going, called "The Poetry Slam," has made it a fun, popular place to come to hear poetry on a Friday night.

3. *tongue-in-cheek*:
   a. badly pronounced
   b. new
   c. difficult to hear
   d. not very serious

. . . the crowd who came to welcome the *Poet Laureate* Joseph Brodsky to the Library of Congress last September . . .

4. *Poet Laureate*:
   a. best poet
   b. official poet
   c. most popular poet
   d. European poet

He wants whole books of poems *racked* right here.

5. *racked*:
   a. written down
   b. given away
   c. displayed for sale
   d. burned

Some *literary* people think Brodsky's *on to something*.

6. *literary*:
   a. strange or unusual
   b. common or ordinary
   c. connected with literature
   d. unfamiliar with literature

7. *is on to something*:
   a. has a good idea
   b. has a bad idea
   c. has the wrong idea
   d. worries about things too much

Just to *down-market* a book because it is a good book and you want to reach the broadest possible audience, I'm afraid, is not a reality today.

8. *down-market*:
   a. sell for a cheaper price
   b. sell for a higher price
   c. sell in outdoor markets
   d. sell downtown

. . . but at a $15 to $22 price, [they are] *a far cry from* Brodsky's books for a *buck* or two.

9. *a far cry from*:
   a. very similar to
   b. completely different from
   c. much sadder than
   d. much louder than

10. *buck*:
    a. young person
    b. penny
    c. short poem
    d. dollar

WORD PUZZLE

1. Unscramble the letters to make a word to fit the definition. All the words are used on the video.
   1. to hate or greatly dislike (hotale) __loathe__
   2. a place where a collection of books is kept (raribly) __Library__
   3. to print and offer for sale to the public (sluphib) __Publish__
   4. a hotel for people who are traveling by car (lemot) __hotel__
   5. places where you can buy newspapers (dasewnstns) __newstands__
   6. large (samevis) __massive__
   7. writers of books, plays and so forth (stroahu) __authors__
   8. a place where you can buy bread and cake (krebay) __bakery__

DISCUSSION

Work in groups. Discuss your answers to the following questions.

1. Were you surprised by anything you saw or heard on the video? If so, what?
2. Has watching this video changed your view of poetry? If so, how? If not, which of your views did the video confirm or strengthen?
3. Name a poet that you studied at school. What do you know about him or her?
4. Many people think that the lyrics of some pop songs are poetry. Do you agree? Explain your answer.

ROLE PLAY

Work in groups of five or six. One student will play the role of the poet. The other students will play the role of members of the audience. Read the situation and role descriptions below and decide who will play which roles. Then change roles – with another student playing the role of the poet – and do the role play again. Keep changing roles until everyone in the group has had a chance to be the poet.

SITUATION: **A Poetry Reading**

You and your classmates have been invited to read and listen to some poetry at the Nuyorican Poets' Cafe.

ROLE DESCRIPTION: **Poet**

You have been invited to read a poem at the Nuyorican Poets' Cafe. Select a short poem in simple English and recite it for the audience at the cafe. It can be your own poem or a poem by another author. Be prepared to answer questions people in the audience might ask about the meaning of the poem.

ROLE DESCRIPTION: **Members of the Audience**

You have come to the Nuyorican Poets Cafe to listen to some poetry. Listen to the poem that the poet reads and then ask the poet questions about the theme and meaning of the poem. Here are some examples of questions you might ask:

Who wrote the poem?

Why did you choose to recite this particular poem?

Does the poem have any personal significance for you?

READING

[handwritten top margin: been gut (get) / belly (bell)]

The poem below was presented later in the program. Read the poem and answer the questions that follow. Then compare your answers with those of another student.

Homage to My Hips

These hips are big hips.
They need space to move around in.
They don't fit into little petty places.
These hips are free hips.
They don't like to be held back.
These hips have never been enslaved.
They go where they want to go,
they do what they want to do.
These hips are mighty hips.
These hips are magic hips. → *[handwritten: magic.]*
I have know them to put a spell on a man,
And to spin him like a top.

1. Which words and phrases in the poem express the following themes?
   a. Big is strong: *[handwritten: these lipps are big hips]*

   b. Big is sexy: *[handwritten: these lips are magic lips]*

   c. Big is liberated: *[handwritten: these lips have never been enslaved.]*

2. Is the writer a man or a woman? How do you know?
   [handwritten: is a woman.]

3. Do you think the poem is meant to be read silently or spoken? Give reasons for your answer.
   [handwritten: spoken]

4. What kind of a person do you imagine the poet to be?
   [handwritten: proud, liberated, sexy,]

5. What does the poet want to say? State the poem's main idea in your own words.

WRITING

Complete one of the following activities.

1. Do you have a favorite poem? Write it down. Then write a summary of the poem.

2. You are Miguel Algarin, one of the founders of the Nuyorican Poets' Cafe. You are preparing a press release for a local newspaper, describing the cafe and how successful "The Poetry Slam" has been. Write 100–150 words describing what an evening at the cafe is like and how audiences respond to the poetry that is read there.

Segment 7
Why Girls Lose Self-Confidence in Their Teens

From: *World News Tonight*, 4/27/93
Begin: 37:39
Length: 5:14

BEFORE YOU WATCH

TALKING POINTS

Work in groups of all males and all females. Discuss your answers to the following questions.

1. At about what age did you first become aware of the opposite sex?

2. What changes, if any, occurred in your relationships with boys/girls at that time?

3. What changes, if any, did you notice in your attitude toward your academic achievements? your social success? the way you dressed? your self-presentation?

PREDICTING

Work in groups. Based on the title of the video segment, *Why Girls Lose Self-Confidence in Their Teens*, write down three questions you think will be answered on the video.

1. _____

2. _____

3. _____

KEY WORDS

The *italicized* words and phrases in the sentences below will help you understand the video. Study the sentences. Then write your own definition of each word or phrase.

1. She's really very talented, but she doesn't have much *self-confidence*.

   self-confidence: _____

2. She was disappointed because she was not *taken seriously*.

   taken seriously: _____

3. She was criticized so much that she began to lose *self-esteem*.

   self-esteem: _____

4. How many *guys* are in your English class?

   guys: _____

5. She spent her *adolescence* in Spain.

   adolescence: _____

6. Boys and girls *mature* sexually during their teens.

   mature: _____

7. He seemed shy and nervous; I don't think he is very *self-assured*.

   self-assured: _____

8. I was surprised she didn't say anything about the problem. She's usually more *outspoken*.

   outspoken: _____

9. Doctors said the young women were suffering from eating *disorders*.

   disorders: _____

10. People who are extremely depressed may have *suicidal tendencies*.

    suicidal tendencies: _____

WHILE YOU WATCH

37:54–
42:32

GETTING THE MAIN IDEA

Watch the news report and listen for the answers to the following questions. Take brief notes on the answers. Then compare your answers with those of another student.

Who is feeling **what**?
Why and **how** can they overcome this?

Who?	
What?	
Why?	
How overcome?	

CHECKING YOUR PREDICTIONS

Look at the questions you wrote in the PREDICTING exercise on page 61. Watch the video. Which of your questions are answered on the video? What answers are given?

37:54–
42:32

WHAT'S MISSING?

Listen to Peter Jennings's introduction to the news report. Fill in the missing words.

37:54–
38:18

Peter Jennings: Finally, this evening on the *American Agenda*, our

(1) _____. Tomorrow at many (2) _____ around

the country, parents are going to take their daughters to

(3) _____. It's the idea of a (4) _____ organization

called the "Ms. Foundation," and the point is to show girls

their future (5) _____ in the (6) _____ to help

(7) _____ them that they are taken (8) _____.

Our Agenda reporter, Carole Simpson, on why girls, in particular,

need such a message.

CHECKING WHAT YOU HEAR

Watch the next part of the news report. What things did the girls associate with the idea of being a man? Check (✔) the appropriate boxes.

38:20–
39:00

1. ❑ power
2. ❑ intelligence
3. ❑ suicidal tendencies
4. ❑ hard work
5. ❑ getting want you want easily
6. ❑ depression

LISTENING FOR DETAILS

Watch the video. Circle the correct answers.

39:38–
41:18

1. As girls mature sexually, they get the message that the ideal woman is expected to
   a. do anything she wants to do.
   b. talk a lot.
   c. be seen more than heard.

2. Fourth-grade girls feel
   a. powerless.
   b. self-assured.
   c. low self-esteem.

3. Eighth-grade girls feel that
   a. textbooks aren't written for them.
   b. they are poorly represented in textbooks.
   c. textbooks are too hard for them.

4. Eighth-grade girls also feel that their teachers
   a. usually favor them in class.
   b. usually criticize them in class.
   c. usually overlook them in class.

5. Eighth-grade girls have low self-esteem
   a. both inside and outside the classroom.
   b. only outside the classroom.
   c. only inside the classroom.

NOTETAKING

Imagine you are a researcher. Watch the video and complete your research notes by filling in the form below. Then compare your notes with those of another student.

39:49–
42:25

1. Most girls are confident up to age _____ or _____.
2. As girls _____, they lose self-esteem.
3. Factors causing the loss of self-esteem are

   _____

   _____

   _____

4. Loss of self-esteem in adolescence can lead to

_____

_____

_____

5. Research shows that mothers can help their daughters by

_____

_____

_____

TRUE OR FALSE?

Watch the next part of the video. Are the following statements *true* or *false*? Write **T** (true) or **F** (false). Make the false statements true by changing one or two words.

41:19–
42:25

1. _____ One reason for teenage pregnancies and eating disorders is the stress girls experience by trying to meet unrealistic expectations.

2. _____ Experts believe that mothers can help build their daughters' self-confidence.

3. _____ Rebecca Klasfeld says she is weaker than some of the boys in her class.

4. _____ Rebecca's mother is teaching Rebecca to be nice and quiet.

5. _____ Rebecca's mother shows her daughter how she is valued.

6. _____ Marie Wilson thinks we should teach girls how they should look, not what they should do.

AFTER YOU WATCH

LANGUAGE POINT: TALKING ABOUT IMAGINARY CONDITIONS

On the video, the teacher is asking about an imaginary condition when she says, "*If* you *were* a boy, *would* they *expect* you to do different things around the house?" When talking about imaginary or unreal conditions, we use the *simple past tense* in the "if" clause, and *would + the simple form of the verb* in the result clause.

Complete the sentences below with the correct forms of the verbs in parentheses. The first one has been done for you.

1. The news report suggests that if American TV commercials (present) __*presented*__ more realistic images of women, teenage girls (be) __*would be*__ more self-assured.

2. In other words, if expectations for women (be) _____ more realistic, the teenagers (feel) _____ more comfortable being themselves.

3. Experts say that girls (have) _____ more self-esteem if their mothers (teach) _____ them to be themselves.

4. If mothers (focus) _____ on their daughters' abilities, not their looks, the girls (feel) _____ more powerful.

5. Experts also believe that if women (be) _____ better represented in textbooks, female students (be) _____ more self-confident both inside and outside class.

6. They also think that girls (participate) _____ more actively in class if they (get) _____ more attention from teachers.

VOCABULARY CHECK

The excerpts below are from the video. What do the *italicized* words mean? Circle the answer that is closest in meaning.

1. Daughters are *anchored* in powerful relationships with us.
   a. made pretty and quiet
   b. separated and lost
   c. made tired and angry
   d. connected and given security

2. They begin to get messages about how to be in the world if they're going to be *accepted* as women.
   a. ruined
   b. disliked
   c. approved
   d. rejected

3. I get really *aggravated* when people tell me that I can't do something.
   a. lazy
   b. annoyed
   c. happy
   d. interested

4. Girls begin to feel *minimized* by textbooks . . .
   a. reduced in importance
   b. increased in importance
   c. stimulated
   d. satisfied

5. . . . and by teachers who still *call on* them less frequently than boys.
   a. ask (them) to participate
   b. telephone
   c. make (them) feel afraid
   d. collect

6. There's this voice in my head telling me, "You know the answer and you can *verbalize* it well . . ."
   a. hear
   b. say
   c. spell
   d. increase

7. . . . and then there's this other voice saying, "Well, it's not going to *come out* right."
   a. sound
   b. leave
   c. disappear
   d. change

8. Experts say the fear of not *living up to* unrealistic expectations is to blame.
   a. enjoying or liking
   b. refusing or declining
   c. meeting or reaching
   d. having or experiencing

9 . . . a typical nine-year-old girl, *full of spunk*.
   a. very sad
   b. very noisy
   c. filled with self-doubt
   d. very self-assertive

10. Rebecca's mom is *struggling* not to teach her daughter what she and most women say they learned from their mothers.
    a. organizing people
    b. trying hard
    c. running slowly
    d. losing weight

DISCUSSION

Work in groups. Discuss your answers to the following questions.

1. In what ways are the teenage and younger girls on the video similar to girls of their age in your culture? In what ways, if any, are they different?

2. According to the video, American TV commercials deliver the message that "the ideal woman is meant to be seen more than heard." What about in your culture? What qualities is the "ideal woman" generally expected to have? Do you agree with your culture's concept of the ideal woman? Why or why not?

3. On the video, Carole Simpson says that girls feel "minimized" by textbooks. In what ways might textbooks minimize women? Can you find any examples in your textbooks for English or other subjects?

ROLE PLAY

Work in groups of three: two females and one male, or two males and one female. The member of the minority sex will play the role of the moderator. The members of the majority sex will be interviewed by the moderator. Read the situation and role descriptions below. After a ten-minute preparation, begin the panel discussion.

THE SITUATION: **A Panel Discussion**

A panel discussion is being held at a conference on "How to Help Teenagers to Develop Self-Confidence."

ROLE DESCRIPTION: **Moderator**

You are the moderator of the panel discussion. Prepare a list of questions relating to teenagers and their self-confidence, and why and how they feel teenagers of their own sex can be helped to develop self-esteem. Conduct the interview. Encourage the use of examples and individual experiences to support personal views.

ROLE DESCRIPTION: **Members of the Panel**

You are being interviewed. Think of situations in which you did not feel confident as a teenager. Be prepared to answer questions about how your life as a teenager could have been made easier and to offer suggestions on how teenagers of your own sex might be helped to gain self-confidence.

READING

Read the article below to find out about the history of feminism in the 1960s. Then answer the questions that follow.

THE FIGHT FOR WOMEN'S RIGHTS IN THE '60S

The protest movement and the fight for women's rights grew out of the struggles of African-Americans and the civil rights movement. In the 1950s most women were expected to get married and become housewives. There were few childcare facilities for mothers who wanted to work outside the home, and women who worked usually earned less than men in the same jobs. Many careers were effectively closed to women. Sexual harassment was not uncommon, but it was not considered a problem – by men.

The black civil rights movement began in 1955 when a black woman, Rosa Parks, in Montgomery, Alabama sat in the "Whites Only" section of a bus. This started off a huge protest movement that led in the sixties to the end of segregation between blacks and whites.

It also led to a revival of the women's movement. Many better-off black and white women were feeling frustrated with their situation – comfortable but powerless. Then a journalist, Betty Friedan, published a book called *The Feminine Mystique*. Betty Friedan was one of a number of women who had been appointed by President John F. Kennedy to sit on state and federal commissions established to examine the status of women in the United States.

In 1966 this group of women attended a conference of the Equal Employment Opportunity Commission. Angry and frustrated at the way women's issues were being ignored, they gathered in Betty Friedan's hotel room and created the National Organization of Women (NOW).

The work of the NOW organization received a lot of publicity. It lobbied Congress about sex discrimination. It filed complaints against the New York Times newspaper for its sex-segregated job advertisements, and it lobbied airlines that forced female flight attendants (but not male flight attendants) to retire when they got married or reached the age of 32.

NOW's main achievement was to raise the consciousness of women. College-educated women in the United States and in Europe in the 1960s began to expect more from life than being second to men. Yet, they felt trapped in their traditional role of looking after men and seeking male attention and approval. Even in 1967 women found that feminist resolutions were dropped from the agenda of a Chicago conference on "new" politics.

Two major decisions in the 1970s in the United States moved women closer to achieving the freedom they were seeking. The first was in 1972 when the U.S. Senate approved a Constitutional amendment that assured equal rights for women by making sexual discrimination an offense. (In fact, all laws passed by Congress have to be ratified by the state legislatures, and in 1982 the Equal Rights Amendment was defeated.) The second was in 1973 when the U.S. Supreme Court decision in the case of *Roe* vs. *Wade* gave women the legal right to choose an abortion. Women still had to fight against sexual discrimination, but at least the law was beginning to protect their rights.

1. What was the name of the woman whose action began the black civil rights movement in 1955?

   _____

2. What book became an important document for women's liberation?

   _____

3. Do you think J.F. Kennedy was for or against women's liberation?

   _____

4. Where and when was the National Organization of Women founded?

   _____

5. What are some practices that NOW campaigners protested against?

   _____

6. Was feminism in the 1960s a working class or middle class issue?

   _____

7. In what year did the U.S. Senate pass an amendment outlawing sex discrimination ? Why and when did this amendment later fall?

   _____

8. What did the *Roe* vs. *Wade* decision allow women to do legally?

WRITING

Complete one of the following activities.

1. You work for an advertising agency. Write the text for a TV commercial that urges *men* to look fit and trim, dress better, and be more physically attractive.

2. Andrea is a newspaper columnist who answers letters from people with personal problems. Read the letter below and decide what advice you would give to the reader. Then write a reply, using what you have learned from the video.

Ask Andrea
Andrea answers your problems

Dear Andrea,

I am worried about my teenage daughter. In the past five years she has changed from a happy and confident 9-year-old to a nervous 14-year-old who lacks self-esteem. She is doing poorly in school and is extremely thin for her age. No matter what she eats, she just seems to lose weight. What should I do?

B.L.

Segment 8
Hillary Rodham Clinton

From: *World News Tonight*, 9/24/93
Begin: 42:56
Length: 5:11
Note: This section is not closed captioned

BEFORE YOU WATCH

TALKING POINTS

Work in groups. Discuss your answers to the following questions.

1. Who is the Head of State in the country in which you were born? Is this person a king? a queen? a president? a prime minister? something else?

2. Is the Head of State in the country in which you were born married? If so, what is the name of his or her spouse (wife or husband)? Does his or her spouse have a job? If so, what is it? Is the job official or unofficial?

3. Many people believe that the wife or husband of a Head of State should not be part of the government. Do you agree? Why or why not?

PREDICTING

The video is about Hillary Rodham Clinton, the wife of Bill Clinton, the 42nd president of the United States. Predict the kinds of information you think will be included on the video.

1. _____

2. _____

3. _____

4. _____

5. _____

KEY WORDS

The following words are used on the video. Which words do you think you will hear together? Match the words on the left with the words in the box. The first one has been done for you.

1. health _care_

2. public _____

3. law _____

4. traditional _____

5. living _____

6. two-person _____

7. presidential _____

8. commencement _____

confirmation
~~care~~
wife
proof
job
address
school
campaign

WHILE YOU WATCH

43:11–48:00

GETTING THE MAIN IDEA

Watch the video and listen for the answers to the following questions. Take brief notes on the answers. Then compare your answers with those of another student.

Who is Hillary Rodham Clinton?

What is she trying to accomplish?

How does the public feel about her work?

Who?
What?
How?

CHECKING YOUR PREDICTIONS

Look at your answers to the questions in the PREDICTING exercise on pages 71 and 72. Watch the video again and check (✔) the kinds of information that are actually included on the video.

43:11–
48:00

WHAT'S MISSING?

Listen to Peter Jennings's introduction to the news report. Fill in the missing words.

43:11–
43:25

Peter Jennings: Finally this evening, our Person of the Week. It is one of the more (1) _____ choices we've made in the last several years. Earlier this week, it (2) _____ to us that this particular (3) _____ had come an (4) _____ long way in the last (5) _____ or so. And then we thought — no, maybe it's the (6) _____ which has come a long way.

CHECKING WHAT YOU HEAR

Watch the next part of the news report. What kind of person does President Bill Clinton say was needed to reform the U.S. health care system? Check (✔) the phrases he uses.

43:32–
43:48

1. ❏ a talented navigator
2. ❏ an obedient individual
3. ❏ a registered Democrat
4. ❏ an experienced lawyer
5. ❏ someone with a rigorous mind
6. ❏ (someone with) a steady compass
7. ❏ (someone with) children
8. ❏ (someone with) a caring heart

LISTENING FOR DETAILS

Watch the next part of video. Circle the correct answers.

44:01–
46:24

1. How does Hillary Clinton describe her experience working with her husband?
   a. She says it's been wonderful.
   b. She says she's excited about it.
   c. Both a and b.

2. How long has Hillary Clinton worked with her husband?
   a. Since they were in high school together.
   b. Since they were in law school together.
   c. Since her husband was elected president.

3. According to Peter Jennings, what do people who know Hillary Clinton well find it hard to imagine?
   a. That she will be able to reform the health care system.
   b. That she would act like the traditional wife of a politician.
   c. Both a and b.

4. According to historian Henry Grass, which of the following is true?
   a. The U.S. presidency is a one-person job.
   b. The U.S. presidency is a two-person job.
   c. Hillary Clinton is really the U.S. president.

5. What work did Hillary Clinton do in the state of Arkansas?
   a. She ran for political office.
   b. She worked to make children healthier.
   c. She campaigned for her father.

6. According to Peter Jennings, which of the following is NOT true?
   a. Hillary Clinton understands politics.
   b. Hillary Clinton keeps the "naysayers" out of the political process.
   c. Hillary Clinton has won the respect of her adversaries.

7. What does Senator Connie Mack say about Hillary Clinton?
   a. That she deserves credit for doing a good job.
   b. That she has impressed both Republicans and Democrats.
   c. Both a and b.

8. What was Hillary Clinton's attitude toward the Gennifer Flowers affair?
   a. "Let's get on with the campaign."
   b. "I'll stand by my man like Tammy Wynette."
   c. "I'll leave my husband."

9. In order to help her husband win the presidency, what did Hillary Clinton decide to do?
   a. Become a "stay-at-home" wife.
   b. Play a less prominent role in the campaign.
   c. Make more speeches about policy.

10. What are Americans saying about Hillary Clinton?
    a. That she is the power on the throne.
    b. That she is the power behind the throne.
    c. That she is the power beside the throne.

NOTETAKING

46:25–
47:10

Watch the next part of the video and take brief notes on the answers to the following questions. Then compare your notes with those of another student.

1. What two adjectives does Peter Jennings use to describe Hillary Clinton?

   _____

2. What does Don Jones say Hillary Clinton has a burning desire to do?

   _____

3. What is the first student's impression of President Clinton?

   _____

4. What is the first student's impression of Mrs. Clinton?

   _____

5. What does the second student say Mrs. Clinton "does a lot of"?

   _____

TRUE OR FALSE?

47:11–
47:55

Watch the last part of the video. Are the following statements about Hillary Clinton *true* or *false*? Write **T** (true) or **F** (false). Make the false sentences true by changing one or two words.

1. _____ She is shown speaking to a group of graduating students.
2. _____ She spoke to the students about her husband's feelings.
3. _____ She was a student at Wellesley College in 1969.
4. _____ She gave a commencement address at Wellesley College.
5. _____ She gave the commencement address in 1989.
6. _____ The president of Wellesley College chose her to make the address.
7. _____ In her speech at Wellesley College, she said that the art of politics was to make possible what appears to be impossible.
8. _____ She and her husband are trying to revolutionize the American political system.

AFTER YOU WATCH

LANGUAGE POINT: REPORTED SPEECH

When you want to report what another person has said, you can use either a *direct quotation* or *reported speech*. Study the examples on the top of page 76.

DIRECT QUOTATION	REPORTED SPEECH
Peter Jennings said, "Mrs. Clinton *is* a very religious, motivated woman."	Peter Jennings said (that) Mrs. Clinton *was* a very religious, motivated woman.
Mrs. Clinton said, "I *want* to be idealistic."	Mrs. Clinton said (that) *she wanted* to be idealistic.

Rewrite these sentences. Change the direct quotations to reported speech.

1. Peter Jennings said, "Mrs. Clinton's passion for health care is undeniably deep."

   _____

   _____

2. Senator Mack said, "I give Hillary credit for a tremendous job."

   _____

   _____

3. He also said, "She has impressed Democrats and Republicans alike."

   _____

   _____

4. A student said, "President Clinton is like the actor, and Mrs. Clinton is like the director."

   _____

   _____

5. Mrs. Clinton said, "I have always tried to keep those feelings with me."

   _____

   _____

6. She also said, "I want to care about the world."

   _____

   _____

VOCABULARY CHECK

The *italicized* words are used on the video. Cross out the word or phrase in each row that *does not* have a similar meaning to the word in *italics*. The first one has been done for you.

1. *traditional*   customary   ~~unusual~~   typical
2. *liberated*   emancipated   made free   confined
3. *adversaries*   friends   enemies   opponents
4. *allegations*   charges   claims   denials
5. *threatened*   protected   endangered   terrorized
6. *alienate*   antagonize   make hostile   delight
7. *glimpse*   glance   quick look   stare
8. *impressions*   mistakes   opinions   thoughts
9. *idealistic*   utopian   visionary   practical
10. *revolutionize*   change   ignore   reform

WORD FORMS

Many adjectives in English have corresponding *adverb forms*. Study these sentences:

Adjective: Mrs. Clinton is a *tireless* worker.
Adverb: Mrs. Clinton works *tirelessly*.

The excerpts below are from the video. Complete each sentence with the adjective or adverb form of the word in parentheses, whichever is correct. Then watch the video and check your answers.

1. It occurred to us that this particular individual had come an (awful) _awfully_ long way in the last year or so.

2. It would have been unthinkable for her to play the (traditional) _____ wife of a politician.

3. She has been (positive) _____ liberated.

4. Mrs. Clinton's passion for health care is (undeniable) _____ deep.

5. She apologized and stepped (deliberate) _____ into her candidate husband's shadow.

6. In attempting to (complete) _____ revolutionize the American health care system, she and her husband are attempting just that.

DISCUSSION

Work in groups. Discuss your answers to the following questions.

1. Were you surprised or shocked by anything you saw or heard on the video? If so, what?
2. Do you agree with the idea expressed on the video that "the presidency is a two-person job at the top"? Explain your answer.
3. In what ways is Hillary Clinton similar to the wives of other important politicians? In what ways is she different?
4. In your opinion, was it a good idea for President Clinton to put Hillary Clinton in charge of reforming the American health care system? Give reasons for your answer.
5. Would you like to meet Hillary Clinton? Why or why not?

ROLE PLAY

Work in pairs. One student will play the role of the interviewer. The other will play the role of Hillary Rodham Clinton. Read the situation and the role descriptions below and decide who will play each role. After a ten-minute preparation, begin the interview.

SITUATION: **A Radio Interview**

> A radio program called "ABC Interviews" has invited Hillary Rodham Clinton to talk about her work and her attempt to reform the American health care system.

ROLE DESCRIPTION: **Interviewer**

> You are the interviewer for "ABC Interviews." Prepare a list of questions to ask Hillary Rodham Clinton about her health care work, her role in government, and her attitude toward change. Consider why she is interested in health care, what she is doing, what difficulties she has with her job, and whether she thinks it is right for the president's wife to hold an important position in government.

ROLE DESCRIPTION: **Hillary Rodham Clinton**

> You are Hillary Rodham Clinton. Be prepared to answer questions about your concern with health care, your work in this area, and whether you feel it is right for the president's wife to hold an important position in government.

READING

Read the passage below to find out more about health care in the United States and the attempt to reform the system. Then answer the questions that follow.

HEALTH INSURANCE FOR EVERYONE

In Britain they have the National Health Service. In the United States they have health insurance. But health care in the United States is expensive, and if you do not have health insurance, your hospital bills could make you bankrupt. In addition, many Americans are not covered by any health insurance. That is why the U.S. health care system needs to be reformed. President Clinton described health care as "the biggest problem I ever messed with." Why is health care such a big problem?

One thing that makes it such a headache is its cost. Since 1980 the cost of health care in the United States has more than quadrupled. Medicines and medical services use up one dollar out of every seven that is spent. Health care costs in the United States are nearly twice as expensive as they are in Britain, Germany, or Japan. Because Americans have to pay such high prices for health care, you might expect them to be healthier than the people in those other countries, but that is not the case. The United States pays super power prices for health care, yet its health standards are no better than those in other developed countries.

In a recent speech, President Clinton shocked his audience when he said that, with the exception of Bolivia and Haiti, the United States has the lowest immunization records in the Western Hemisphere. According to a BBC report, the polio vaccine that costs up to $10 per person in the United States cost only $1.87 per person in Britain. For some reason, pharmaceuticals – even those discovered and produced in the United States – cost far less in Canada, Europe, and Mexico.

How is it possible that the richest country on earth does not provide basic health care for everyone? Why do more than 37 million Americans have no health insurance at all? That is what the president's wife, Hillary Rodham Clinton, has to find out. Her task is to find a way to provide universal health care coverage at high standards but at a lower cost. Increased taxes on things like cigarettes will help raise enough money to pay for insurance for all Americans, and private health insurance companies will offer an insurance umbrella to everyone. The aim is to design a plan under which no one will be refused health insurance.

The health care reform will affect everyone in the United States – from millionaires to the poorest farmers. If it succeeds, it will be the greatest reform since the New Deal, the social and economic program that President Franklin Delano Roosevelt launched in 1933.

1. How do health care costs in Britain, Germany, and Japan compare with those in the United States?

_____

2. How do the standards of health care in the United States compare with those in other developed countries?

_____

3. Where do drugs and medicines, discovered and manufactured in America, cost less than they do in the United States?

_____

4. How many Americans are without health insurance?

_____

5. What is Hillary Clinton's task?

_____

6. Who will be affected by Bill and Hillary Clinton's reform of health care?

_____

WRITING

Complete one of the following activities.

1. You are a doctor. Write a letter to Hillary Rodham Clinton and explain how the health care system works in the country where you practice.

2. You are an American politician. Write a short speech (150 – 200 words) expressing your own ideas about whether the U.S. presidency is a one- or two-person job. Begin your speech with one of the openings below.

   The presidency is a two-person job. The president's wife should have a job in government . . .

   The American people elected the president, not his wife. Why does she have a job in government?

Segment 9

PG & E Trains Women for Construction and "Men's" Jobs

From: *World News Tonight,* 2/10/93
Begin: 48:10
Length: 5:18

BEFORE YOU WATCH

TALKING POINTS

Work in groups. Discuss your answers to the following questions.

1. What different kinds of jobs have you done in your life (even for a short time)? Which of them do you consider to be "men's" jobs? Which do you consider to be "women's" jobs? Which are both? Complete the following chart:

Some Jobs I've Had		
"Men's" Jobs	"Men's" or "Women's" Jobs	"Women's" Jobs
_____	_____	_____
_____	_____	_____
_____	_____	_____
_____	_____	_____

2. Why do some people think women are better at some jobs and men are better at others?

3. Do you think people should be given the opportunity to work at jobs that are non-traditional for their sex? Explain your answer.

PREDICTING

The video is about training women to work in "men's" jobs in the construction industry. What difficulties might men and women have with this? List three problems you think will be mentioned on the video.

1. _____

2. _____

3. _____

KEY WORDS

The *italicized* words in the sentences below will help you understand the video. Study the sentences. Then write your own definition of each word.

1. Some female employees accused the company of sex *discrimination*.
   *discrimination:*_____

2. One woman claimed she had experienced sexual *harassment* on the job.
   harassment: _____

3. Until the second half of this century, the fields of business management, law, and medicine were *male-dominated*.
   male-dominated: _____

4. Female employees are still rare in the construction *trades*.
   trades: _____

5. People who work with heavy tools and equipment as part of their job have to be physically *fit*.
   fit: _____

6. *Hands-on* training can help make workers feel more comfortable with new equipment.
   hands on: _____

7. The company is making a special effort to *recruit* female workers.
   recruit: _____

8. In the United States, women and *minorities* now have more and better work opportunities than they have had in the past.
   minorities: _____

WHILE YOU WATCH

GETTING THE MAIN IDEA

Watch the video and listen for the answers to the following questions. Take brief notes on the answers. Then compare your answers with those of another student.

48:25–
52:55

> **Who** is doing **what**, **where**?
> **Why** and **how** are they doing this?

Who?	
What?	
Where?	
Why?	
How?	

CHECKING YOUR PREDICTIONS

Look at the list you made in the PREDICTING exercise on page 82. Check (✔) the problems that are actually mentioned on the video.

48:25–
52:55

WHAT'S MISSING?

Listen to Peter Jennings's introduction to the news report. Fill in the missing words.

48:25–
48:46

Peter Jennings: On the *American Agenda* tonight, (1) _____ it in a man's world if you're a woman. No (2) _____ , there have been changes in the American (3) _____ . People don't look (4) _____ anymore when they see a woman as doctor or (5) _____ or business manager, but there are still a great many jobs that men, at least, go on considering men's (6) _____ . On the *American Agenda* tonight, (7) _____ down another (8) _____ . Our Agenda reporter is Carole Simpson.

WHAT DO YOU SEE

48:46–
49:31

Watch the next part of the video with the sound *off*. Number the following items from 1 to 6 in the order in which you see them. The first one has been done for you.

_____ a female worker lifting boxes

_____ a female worker snipping wire

_____ a female worker snipping parts of a tree

_1_ a female worker climbing a utility pole

_____ workers replacing computer boards

_____ a female worker hanging from a metal construction unit and grabbing a hanging bucket

LISTENING FOR DETAILS

49:06–
50:40

Watch the video. Circle the correct answers.

1. How many jobs in the construction industry are held by women?
   a. More than 10 percent.
   b. About 5 percent.
   c. Less than 3 percent.

2. What does "PG & E" stand for?
   a. Pacific Gas and Electric Corporation.
   b. Pacific Gas and Electric Company.
   c. Pacific Gas and Electricity Construction.

3. When did Felicie Leech start to work at PG & E?
   a. In the early 1980s.
   b. In the mid-1980s.
   c. In the late 1980s.

4. What did Felicie Leech do before she went to work for PG & E?
   a. She was a housewife.
   b. She was a teacher.
   c. She was an apprentice worker.

5. What job does Felicie Leech have at PG & E?
   a. She's an apprentice worker.
   b. She's a salary manager.
   c. She's a construction supervisor.

6. Which statement is NOT true about Felicie Leech's job at PG & E?
   a. It's physically demanding.
   b. It pays less than her old job.
   c. It's dangerous.

7. Is Felicie Leech scared when she's up on a tower?
   a. No, never.
   b. Yes, sometimes.
   c. Yes, always.

8. Has Felicie Leech been exposed to any sexual harassment?
   a. Yes, a lot.
   b. Yes, but only a little.
   c. No, none.

TRUE OR FALSE?

Watch the video. Are the following statements *true* or *false*? Write **T** (true) or **F** (false). Make the false statements true by changing one or two words.

50:51–52:01

1. _____ Fair Start is a pre-employment training program for men.

2. _____ The program prepares trainees for jobs in a traditional field.

3. _____ The training lasts six weeks.

4. _____ The trainees spend an hour a day in physical training.

5. _____ The program includes hands-on training with equipment and tools.

6. _____ PG & E sponsors committees that deal with sexual harassment.

7. _____ Women have quit their jobs because of the committees.

8. _____ There have been no problems with the program.

NOTETAKING

Watch the video and take brief notes on the answers to the following questions. Then compare your answers with those of another student.

51:36–52:38

1. What is Richard Clark's concern?

   _____

   _____

2. In what two ways has the Fair Start program been successful?

   _____

   _____

3. How has the PG & E workforce changed, according to Bob Baker?

   _____

   _____

4. How many female employees does PG & E employ? How many are in non-traditional jobs?

_____

_____

LANGUAGE POINT: USED TO vs. BE USED TO

On the video, when the telephone worker says, "I *used to go* through that . . .", she is talking about how she felt *in the past*. Notice the difference in form and meaning between these two sentences:

I *used to go* there. (= It was my habit to go there *in the past*.)

I *am used to going* there. (= *I am accustomed* to going there.)

Complete each of the following sentences with the most appropriate form: *used to* + base form of the verb or *be used to* + gerund. The first one has been done for you.

1. People in the U.S. (see) __*are used to seeing*__ female doctors and lawyers, but female construction workers are less common.

2. No women (work) _____ in the construction trades, but now some women do.

3. By now male employees at PG & E (work) _____ with women on construction jobs.

4. Most women (feel) _____ they had to be better than men in order to prove themselves, but now many don't feel that way.

5. Now women at PG & E (do) _____ hard physical work, thanks to the training in the Fair Start program.

6. In the old days, women at PG & E (quit) _____ their jobs because of sexual harassment, but the situation has changed.

VOCABULARY CHECK

The *italicized* words are used on the video. Cross out the word or phrase that does not have a similar meaning to the words in *italics*.

1. *barrier*	passage	difficulty	obstacle
2. *hike*	walk	tramp	drive
3. *frail*	delicate	strong	weak

4. *apprentice*	trainee	learner	supervisor
5. *pornographic*	innocent	obscene	lewd
6. *resent*	be angry about	feel good about	feel bitter about
7. *eliminate*	join together	remove	get rid of
8. *fair*	impartial	unequal	equal

WORD FORMS

The sentences below are from the video. <u>Underline</u> the correct word form in each set of parentheses. Then watch the video and check your answers. The first one has been done for you.

1. (Sympathy, Sympathize, <u>Sympathetic</u>) male co-workers try to explain why other men are so (resistance, resist, resistant) to women.
2. I think the guys there (threats, threatened, threatening) and operated from fear, and that makes them do crazy things.
3. It's (devastated, devastate, devastating) to them, and it doesn't help the company.
4. While there are still problems, the program has been successful in preparing the women for jobs and (sensitivity, sensitizing, sensitive) many of the men to the new (reality, realize, real).
5. Only 450 women out of PG & E's 6,000 female employees are doing non-traditional work, but the company is making an effort to (encouragement, encourage, encouraging) more women to try it.
6. Clearly, it's not for everybody, but for women like Felicie Leech, it's the most (satisfaction, satisfy, satisfying) work she's ever done.

COLLOQUIAL EXPRESSIONS

The excerpts below are from the video. What do the *italicized* expressions mean? Study the excerpts. Then match the expressions with the meanings on the following page.

1. On the *American Agenda* tonight, *making it* in a man's world if you're a woman.

2. I used to *go through* that . . . but I really don't feel that way anymore.

3. You don't have to try and be a man, 'cause chances are a lot of time that *works against* you.

4. Felicie said she had to *put up with* a lot of harassment from men.

5. When you *come across* some of the guys that have got 20, 25 years . . .

1. _____ *making it*   a. cause problems for

2. _____ *go through*   b. meet by chance

3. _____ *work against*   c. succeeding

4. _____ *put up with*   d. experience

5. _____ *come across*   e. tolerate or accept

DISCUSSION

Work in groups. Discuss your answers to the following questions.

1. Were you surprised by anything on the video? If so, what?

2. As Peter Jennings points out on the video, Americans "don't look twice when they see a woman as a doctor or lawyer or business manager." Are female doctors, lawyers, and business managers common in your culture? Explain your answer.

3. What jobs in your culture are considered to be "men's work"? What jobs are considered to be "women's work"? Has any effort been made to encourage people to try jobs that are non-traditional for their sex?

ROLE PLAY

Work in pairs. One student will play the role of the employer. The other student will play the role of the job applicant. Read the situation and role descriptions below and decide who will play each role. After a ten-minute preparation, begin the interview.

THE SITUATION: **A Job Interview**

An employer has invited an applicant to be interviewed for a job that is non-traditional for the applicant's sex. Choose one of the following situations (or make up a situation of your own) and plan your role play around it.

a. A woman is applying for a job as a security guard.

b. A man is applying for a job as a housekeeper.

e. A woman is applying for a job as an auto mechanic.

f. A man is applying for a job as a manicurist.

ROLE DESCRIPTION: **Employer**

You are the employer. Make up a list of questions to ask the applicant about his or her education, experience, ability to do the job, and reasons for wanting the job. Be prepared to answer questions about working conditions, salary, and other job-related

88

issues. At the end of the interview, offer the applicant the job or say, "I'll let you know."

ROLE DESCRIPTION: **Job Applicant**

You are the job applicant. Make up a list of questions to ask the employer about working conditions, salary, and other job related issues. Be prepared to answer questions about your education, experience, ability to do the job, and why you want the job. At the end of the interview, decide whether or not to accept the job if it is offered.

READING

Read the article below to find out about an important American feminist writer. then answer the questions that follow.

GLORIA STEINEM, ICON OF THE WOMEN'S MOVEMENT

I was looking forward to interviewing Gloria Steinem, but I was also very nervous about our meeting. Would I be politically correct enough for her? Would I make sexist remarks without thinking? Would she get angry and throw me out of the room?

The room was her suite in Durrants Hotel, a lovely, traditional English hotel in London's West End. She was slim and young looking with beautiful long hair, but her biographical data said she was born in 1934. No, it must have been a mistake. She looked at least twenty years younger. She was gentle, low voiced, and extremely considerate. I thought, "How can such a famous feminist be so feminine?" Wisely, I didn't allow myself to say such a stupid thing. Of course feminism and femininity aren't incompatible.

I first heard of Gloria Steinem in the early 70s when I saw the first issue of *Ms.*

Magazine, the feminist monthly that she founded and edited. When I finally met her in the late 80s, she had just published a book about Marilyn Monroe – a woman who had genuinely tried to realize herself but who had been trapped in her own history and self-view. Gloria Steinem also had to fight against her own self view. In one of her other books, *Revolution From Within: A Book of Self-Esteem*, she revealed that she had been brought up in a rat-infested home and felt neglected as a child. She felt lonely and abandoned. She feared being invisible. As a woman, she feared being fat and she feared getting breast cancer. Part of her importance as a feminist leader is that although she has experienced a great many fears, she has been able to face up to them and share them with others through her writing. As a result, those women who read Steinem's writings feel more secure.

1. What kind of person did the author expect Gloria Steinem to be?

   _____

2. What is she like in reality?

   _____

3. What two people has Gloria Steinem written books about?

   _____

4. What are some words that are used to describe Gloria Steinem's childhood?

   _____

5. What are some fears that Gloria Steinem has had as an adult?

   _____

6. How do you think Gloria Steinem helps other women?

   _____

WRITING

Complete one of the following activities.

1. You are applying for a non-traditional job such as a male nanny, male housekeeper, female auto mechanic, or female plumber. Write a 150–200 word letter of application describing your background and qualifications and say why you think you would be good for the job.

2. You are a personnel manager or educational administrator. Write a nine-point plan to provide equal opportunities for men and women in your school, college, or workplace. The plan is to be posted on notice boards in your school, college, or workplace.

Segment 10
Robert Redford, Sundance Film Festival Founder

From: *World News Tonight,* 1/29/93
Begin: 53:31
Length: 4:44

BEFORE YOU WATCH

TALKING POINTS

Work in groups. Discuss your answers to the following questions.

1. Who is Robert Redford? Make a list of everything you know about him.

2. The titles of some of Robert Redford's movies are printed below. Which, if any, have you seen? Describe what the movie was about.

Butch Cassidy and the Sundance Kid	*The Sting*
The Way We Were	*Sneakers*
All the President's Men	*Legal Eagles*
Indecent Proposal	*The Natural*

3. What do the roles Robert Redford has played in the movies tell you about him?

PREDICTING

Based on the title of video segment, *Robert Redford, Sundance Film Festival Founder*, what do you think you will see and hear on the video? Write down five items under each of the headings that follow. Then compare your answers with those of another student.

SIGHTS	WORDS
(things you expect to see)	(words you expect to hear)

1. _____   _____

2. _____   _____

3. _____   _____

4. _____   _____

5. _____   _____

KEY WORDS

The *italicized* words in the sentences below will help you understand the video. Study the sentences. Then match the words with the meanings.

1. Rice is the *staple* of the diet in many Asian countries.
2. Her style of dress is definitely *offbeat*.
3. He has a *diversity* of interests: she likes travel and music.
4. He is an expert at the *craft* of filmmaking.
5. I wanted to become a movie star, but my film career *fizzled*.
6. The play has just ended a six-week *run* on Broadway.
7. The film wasn't popular in the United States, but it was a big *hit* in Europe.
8. As the successful president of a major international corporation, she has a great deal of economic *clout*.
9. All her life she fought for one *cause*: world peace.
10. The president began the meeting by welcoming the *newcomers*.

1. _____ *staple*   a. ended in a disappointing way

2. _____ *offbeat*   b. power or influence

3. _____ *diversity*   c. a major or very important part

4. _____ *craft*   d. unusual, and often humorous

5. _____ *fizzled*   e. a success

6. _____ *run* (n)   f. variety

7. _____ *hit* (n)   g. an occupation that requires skill

8. _____ *clout*   h. a continuous set of performances

9. _____ *cause* (n)   i. people who have recently arrived at a place, started a job, or joined a group

10. _____ *newcomers*   j. an aim or a movement that a group of people supports

WHILE YOU WATCH

GETTING THE MAIN IDEA

Watch the news report and listen for the answers to the following
questions. Take brief notes on the answers. Then compare your answers
with those of another student.

53:46–
58:12

> **What** is Robert Redford doing? **Where**?
>
> **Why** and **how** is he doing this?
>
> **How long** has he been doing this?

What?	
Where?	
Why?	
How?	
How long?	

CHECKING YOUR PREDICTIONS

Look at the lists you made in the PREDICTING exercise on page 92. Watch
the video and check (✔) the items that you actually see and hear.

53:46–
58:12

WHAT'S MISSING?

Listen to Peter Jennings's introduction to the news report. Fill in the
missing words.

53:46–
54:03

Peter Jennings: Finally, this evening, our Person of the Week –

(1) _____ recognizable to millions of people throughout

the world, a (2) _____ of American culture, and the man

we choose this week, because he has become one of the most

(3) _____ examples of an (4) _____ in a fairly selfish

industry who (5) _____ in giving something

(6) _____.

CHECKING WHAT YOU HEAR

54:04–
55:35

Watch the next part of the news report. Robert Redford and Peter Jennings mention the reasons behind the Sundance Film Festival and Institute. Number the reasons from 1 to 6 in the order in which they are mentioned. The first one has been done for you.

_____ To encourage diversity

_____ To allow new talent to emerge (become known)

__1__ To provide a place for people with independent vision

_____ To give young filmmakers a chance to show their work to distributors and producers with money

_____ To give filmmakers a chance to develop their craft

_____ To give people the opportunity to fail or make mistakes

NOTETAKING

54:30–
55:35

Watch the video again and take brief notes on the answers to the following questions. Then compare your notes with those of another student.

1. How many filmmakers were at the Sundance Film Festival the year this news report was broadcast?

   _____

2. In what state is the festival held?

   _____

3. How important is the festival?

   _____

4. Why do young filmmakers go to the Sundance Film Festival?

   _____

5. How much money did it cost to produce most of the films that were shown at the festival?

   _____

6. What does Robert Redford believe is "the engine" of American culture?

   _____

7. When did Robert Redford first open the Sundance Film Institute?

   _____

8. What does Robert Redford believe in doing?

   _____

LISTENING FOR DETAILS

The next part of the news report gives details of Robert Redford's career. Watch the video and circle the correct answers to the following questions.

55:36–56:15

1. Robert Redford grew up in
   a. New York.
   b. Utah.
   c. Los Angeles.

2. Originally he wanted to be
   a. in the theater.
   b. an artist.
   c. in movies.

3. His career as a painter in Europe was
   a. very successful.
   b. fairly successful.
   c. unsuccessful.

4. His first success as an actor was in
   a. a Broadway theater production of *Barefoot in the Park*.
   b. the film version of *Barefoot in the Park*.
   c. a London theater production of *Barefoot in the Park*.

5. He became a star in
   a. 1957.
   b. 1967.
   c. 1977.

TRUE OR FALSE?

Watch the video. Are the following statements about Robert Redford *true* or *false*? Write **T** (true) or **F** (false). Make the false statements true by changing one or two words.

56:22–58:02

1. _____ Robert Redford had many hit movies in the 1980s.

2. _____ He was a major star by the mid-1970s.

3. _____ He thinks the United States should invest more in solar energy.

4. _____ He is interested in protecting the environment.

5. _____ He stopped making commercial films in the 1990s.

6. _____ He continues to make movies fairly regularly.

7. _____ He uses his name and his money to help others make movies.

6. _____ His most satisfying course at the Sundance Film Institute is the art of acting.

LANGUAGE POINT: PARTICIPLES USED AS ADJECTIVES

On the video, Robert Redford uses the present participle of the verb "satisfy" as an adjective when he says, "The most *satisfying* thing is my main course, which is The Art of Film." *The present and past participles of some verbs can be used as adjectives.* Study the following examples:

Present participle: Robert Redford has had a *fascinating* career.

Past participle: Robert Redford is *fascinated* by filmmaking.

Now complete the following sentences with the appropriate participle of the verb in parentheses.

1. Robert Redford is (interest) _____ in promoting the work of young filmmakers.

2. The Sundance Film Festival is one of the most (excite) _____ festivals in the United States.

3. Robert Redford is most (satisfy) _____ with his Art of Film course.

4. The Sundance Film Institute is a (fascinate) _____ example of putting something back into the industry.

5. Robert Redford is not (surprise) _____ that Hollywood has a merchant mentality.

6. Robert Redford doesn't find it (annoy) _____ that the Hollywood film industry is a business.

VOCABULARY CHECK: COLLOQUIAL EXPRESSIONS

The following excerpts are from the video. What do the *italicized* expressions mean? Circle the answer that is closest in meaning.

1. He has become one of the most visible examples of an artist . . . who believes in *giving something back*.
   a. providing financial support
   b. refusing something
   c. stopping using something
   d. returning something

2. They are mostly young filmmakers who've yet to see their name *in lights*.
   a. on a neon sign
   b. in fireworks
   c. on a birthday cake with candles
   d. on a dressing room door

3. I think the most important thing is diversity, which is what I think has been really the *engine* of our culture.
   a. mechanical tool
   b. driving force
   c. weakness
   d. motorized vehicle

4. It's a place where people could fail because it's very hard to do that in Hollywood because *the meter's ticking*.
   a. the taxi is waiting
   b. it is too noisy
   c. electricity is expensive
   d. there is no time

5. I'm old-fashioned, if you want, but I believe in *putting something back into* an industry that I have taken something out of.
   a. replacing something in
   b. removing something from
   c. contributing something to
   d. selling something to

6. I just kind of *fell into it* naturally.
   a. had an accident with it
   b. went to sleep on it
   c. made a mistake about it
   d. started it without intending to

7. After his painting career fizzled in Europe, . . . he *tried his hand at* Broadway.
   a. waved good-bye
   b. had great success
   c. tested his ability
   d. got tired of working

8. A successful run in Neil Simon's *Barefoot in the Park* in 1973 *led him into* some truly forgettable movies.
   a. got him involved in
   b. saved him from
   c. made him watch
   d. helped him remember

WORD FORMS

The excerpts below are from the video. The *italicized* words are either nouns, verbs, or adjectives. Fill in the chart that follows by adding the other forms of each word. The first one has been done for you. In some categories, there is more than one possibility. When you finish, compare your chart with that of another student.

1. Finally, this evening, our Person of the Week: instantly *recognizable* to millions of people throughout the world . . .
2. But for those people who have independent vision, you know, special stories to tell that are more *risky* . . .
3. It is an opportunity to show and *promote* their work to distributors and producers with money.
4. It's about the *emergence* of new talent.
5. I think the most important thing is *diversity*.
6. Robert Redford . . . certainly never *calculated* that he would be an actor.

7. He *continues* to make movies fairly regularly.
8. The most *satisfying* thing to me . . . the art of film.

NOUN	VERB	ADJECTIVE
recognition	*recognize*	recognizable
		risky
	promote	
emergence		
diversity		
	calculated	
	continues	
		satisfying

DISCUSSION

Work in groups. Discuss your answers to the following questions.

1. Many people say movies are the art of the 20th century. Do you agree? Why or why not?

2. Do you have a favorite movie? If so, what is it? Describe the film to the group.

3. Do you have a favorite movie star? If so, who is it? Explain why you like him or her.

4. Robert Redford says that diversity is the "engine" of American culture. What do you think he means by this?

5. Is diversity an important part of your home country's culture? Explain your answer.

ROLE PLAY: GREAT CAUSES

Robert Redford has supported several causes: solar energy, protecting the environment, and filmmaking. Work in groups of four or five. Select a cause that you and all the other members of your group support. It might be one of the causes that Robert Redford has supported or some other cause, such as fighting world hunger, protecting the rain forests, promoting world peace, or any other cause the group feels is important.

Together, prepare a list of points that will attract supporters to your cause. After a fifteen-minute preparation, present your cause to the class. Follow this procedure:

1. One member of the group describes the cause.

2. Other group members take turns presenting arguments in support of the cause.

3. As groups present their causes, the other members of the class take notes on the cause and the arguments each group presents.

4. After each group has presented its cause, class members vote on the causes they would like to adopt.

READING

Read the following excerpts from a film guide to find out more about Robert Redford's film career. Then answer the questions that follow.

All the President's Men (1976) C-138 minutes. ***: Alan J. Pakula. Robert Redford, Dustin Hoffman, Jason Robards, Jane Alexander, Hal Holbrook.

Redford and Hoffman play real-life *Washington Post* reporters Bob Woodward and Carl Bernstein, who persevered in their investigation of the events that led to the resignation of President Nixon. Redford was also Executive Producer of this great movie, that combines the best elements of newspaper pictures, detective stories and thrillers. Nominated for an Academy Award as Best Picture, it lost to *Rocky*. Jason Robards and screenwriter William Goldman, however, won Oscars for their work.

Butch Cassidy and the Sundance Kid (1969) C-112 minutes. ****: George Roy Hill. Paul Newman, Robert Redford, Katharine Ross, Strother Martin.

Comic westerns usually don't do well at the box office, but this warm, humorous film was an instant hit. Outlaws Newman and Redford are chased by a remote sheriff and his posse. Many memorable scenes. Nominated for Best Picture, Best Director and Sound, it won Oscars for Cinematography, Original Score, Song ("Raindrops Keep Fallin' on My Head"), and Screenplay.

Ordinary People (1980) C-124 minutes. ****: Robert Redford. Donald Sutherland, Mary Tyler Moore, Judd Hirsch, Timothy Hutton.

Superbly adapted from Judith Guest's novel, this powerful film examines relationships within a family from the point of view of the younger son after the accidental death of his older brother. Intelligent and well-crafted, the film made a remarkable directorial debut for Redford and was selected as Best Picture of 1980 by both the National Film Board and the Academy Awards. Other Oscars were awarded to Timothy Hutton (Best Supporting Actor) and to Alvin Sargent (Screenplay). Sutherland deserved, but did not get, a nomination as Best Actor.

War Hunt (1962) B&W-85 minutes. *:Denis Sanders. John Saxon, Robert Redford, Charles Aidman, Sydney Pollack.

This offbeat war story is notable for its good acting, but has little else to recommend it. In Korea in 1953, a kill-crazy soldier (John Saxon) befriends and tries to help a war orphan but finally has to be shot. Redford is impressive in his film debut as a young soldier who witnesses Saxon's heroics. Vaguely interesting but not very effective indictment of the realities of war.

1. In which film did Robert Redford make his acting debut?

   _____

2. Which film listed here did he direct?

   _____

3. In which film did he co-star with Paul Newman?

   _____

4. On which film did he serve as executive producer?

   _____

5. Which film is a comedy?

   _____

6. Which film did the reviewer like the least?

   _____

7. Which film is a true story based on events involving the White House?

   _____

8. Which film won an Academy Award for Best Picture?

   _____

WRITING

Complete one of the following activities.

1. Write a short review (100 – 150 words) of a movie you have seen in a movie theater or on TV. You can use the following questions as a guide.

   What is the title of the film?
   What kind of film is it (drama, comedy, suspense, etc.)?
   What stars appear in the film? What roles do they play?
   Who directed the film?
   What is the story about?
   What is your opinion of the film?
   What things do you particularly like or dislike about the film?
   Do you recommend that other people see this film?
   Why or why not?

2. Write a short article (100 – 150 words) for your school or college newspaper, describing one of the causes presented by your classmates in the role play (not your own cause!). Give your opinion about why people should or should not support the cause.

Segment 11
TV Technology

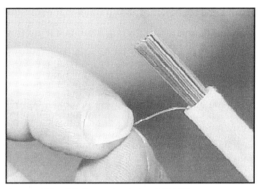

From: *World News Tonight,* 9/28/93
Begin: 58:19
Length: 5:23

BEFORE YOU WATCH

TALKING POINTS

Work in groups. Discuss your answers to the following questions.

1. How many hours of TV do you watch in an average week?
2. What kinds of programs do you like to watch?
3. In what ways has television changed in your lifetime?
4. What recent developments in TV technology are you aware of, if any?
5. Can you think of any ways in which TV could be made more interesting or useful to viewers?

PREDICTING

Work in groups. Based on the title of the news report, *TV Technology*, and the picture above, predict the kinds of information you think will be included in the video.

1. _____

2. _____

3. _____

4. _____

5. _____

KEY WORDS

The *italicized* words in the sentences below will help you understand the news report. Study the sentences. Then match the words with the meanings.

1. How many *channels* can your television set receive?
2. A *superhighway* connects all the cities and towns in the area.
3. We always *tune in* at 10 o'clock to hear the news.
4. Tele-Communications, Inc., is one of the largest *cable TV* companies in the United States.
5. Telephone companies around the nation use *optic fibers* to carry long-distance calls.
6. I think there is a loose *strand* in this wire.
7. All of the major television networks *transmit* news programs.
8. Don't just sit there like a *couch potato*.
9. My television set and VCR can be run by *remote control*.
10. The newer computer models allow for more *interactivity*.

1. _____ *channels*   a. to set a radio or TV to a particular station

2. _____ *superhighway*   b. a single piece or thread in a rope or cable

3. _____ *tune in*   c. television stations

4. _____ *cable TV*   d. threads that use light to carry information

5. _____ *optic fibers*   e. to send out by radio or TV signals

6. _____ *strand*   f. a very large main road

7. _____ *transmit*   g. a lazy person who spends a lot of time just sitting and watching TV

8. _____ *couch potato*   h. devices used to operate machines from a distance

9. _____ *remote control*   i. two-way communication between machines and the people who use them

10. _____ *interactivity*   j. a type of system that transmits television signals by wire

WHILE YOU WATCH

GETTING THE MAIN IDEA

58:34–
1:03:23

Watch the news report and listen for the answers to the following questions. Take brief notes on the answers. Then compare your answers with those of another student.

Who is doing **what**, **where**?
Why and **how** are they doing this?

Who?	
What?	
Where?	
Why?	
How?	

CHECKING YOUR PREDICTIONS

Look at your answers to the PREDICTING exercise on page 101. Watch the video again. Did you learn what you expected to from the video?

58:34–
1:03:23

WHAT'S MISSING?

Listen to Peter Jennings's introduction to the news report. Fill in the missing words.

58:34–
59:05

Peter Jennings: On the *American Agenda* tonight, the (1) _____ in your living room. Most all of us who watch television — not to mention those of us who work in it — have at least the sense that the whole television (2) _____ is shifting under our feet. On this (3) _____, for example, we sometimes wonder not how, but (4) _____ we will fit in the new world of 500 (5) _____. And we're as (6) _____ as anyone. So we asked our media analyst, Jeff Greenfield, to spend the next three nights guiding us down this new (7) _____ superhighway so that we may know better how to (8) _____ in tomorrow.

LISTENING FOR DETAILS

Watch the video. Circle the correct answers.

59:06–
1:01:01

1. In 1939, what did people predict many buildings would have in 1960?
   a. Cable TV receivers.
   b. Landing decks for helicopters.
   c. Both a and b.

2. In 1964, what did people think we would be using by now?
   a. Electronically run vehicles.
   b. Interactive computer systems.
   c. An information superhighway.

3. According to the news report, what is the most commonly shared experience of American life?
   a. Traveling by automobile.
   b. Knocking on people's front doors.
   c. Watching television.

4. According to the news report, what is being reinvented?
   a. Television.
   b. The telephone.
   c. Both a and b.

5. How many channels are cable TV customers in parts of New York already equipped to receive?
   a. 50.
   b. 150.
   c. 500.

6. What does Jeff Greenfield predict will be common within a few years?
   a. Cable systems with 500 channels.
   b. Cable channels aimed at viewers' narrower tastes.
   c. Both a and b.

7. How is the new TV technology different from the old?
   a. Viewers tell their TV sets what they want to see.
   b. Viewers tell their TV sets when they want to see something.
   c. Both a and b.

8. What is the key to the revolution in TV technology?
   a. Optic fiber cables.
   b. Moving information back and forth between viewer and TV.
   c. Transmitting the *Encyclopedia Britannica*.

CHECKING WHAT YOU HEAR

1:01:23–
1:02:29

Watch the next part of the video. How is television changing? Check (✔) the things that the report says users of new TV technology can already do, or will be able to do in the near future.

1. ❏ Dial up any database, theater, library, church, or university classroom

2. ❏ Push a button to get information about a baseball player's statistics

3. ❑ Tell their TV sets what kinds of programs they want to see

4. ❑ Use remote controls to preview, order, and pay for TV shows

5. ❑ Use remote controls to get information about a friend's salary

6. ❑ Play video games with a friend who lives across town

7. ❑ Use their TVs to examine and order goods they want to buy

8. ❑ Use their TVs to call up health records

9. ❑ Receive and send work from their homes via TV

10. ❑ Have a two-way conversation with the vice-president

TRUE OR FALSE?

Watch the video. Are the following statements *true* or *false*? Write **T** (true) or **F** (false). Make the false statements true by changing one or two words.

1:02:30– 1:03:19

1. _____ Vice-President Gore hopes the new TV technology will encourage children to play more video games.

2. _____ Vice-President Gore believes the new technology should respond to a child's imagination.

3. _____ There is very little we don't know about the new TV technology.

4. _____ We know how much interactivity viewers want.

5. _____ We know how much it is going to cost.

6. _____ We know who is going to control the information superhighway.

AFTER YOU WATCH

LANGUAGE POINT: VERBS FOLLOWED BY PREPOSITIONS

Some English verbs are followed by specific prepositions. The excerpts below are from the video. Fill in each blank with the correct preposition from the box. Some of the prepositions are used more than once. When you have finished, watch the video and check your answers.

for	into	on	up
from	like	out	to

1. We don't always know what the future is going to look _____.

2. But when it comes _____ the most commonly shared experience of American life — watching television — there's no doubt that the future is not just around the corner, but knocking _____ the front door.

3. Cable customers in parts of New York are already wired _____ 150 channels.

4. The real story is that the whole nature of television is changing _____ a one-way communication system to a world where you tell your TV set what you want to see, when you want to see it.

5. The features of cable TV, the telephone, and the computer are all converging _____ one device — one that makes it possible to tap _____ an apparently limitless universe of entertainment and information.

6. You'll be able to dial _____ any database, theater, library, church, any university classroom.

7. Viewers watching the baseball game can push a button on their remote controls and call _____ a player's statistics, even his salary.

8. And some cable systems are already trying _____ video on demand.

9. You preview it and order and pay _____ it with a click of your remote control.

10. I want to see a time when a school child can come home after class, and instead of playing a video game, plug _____ the Library of Congress.

VOCABULARY CHECK

The *italicized* words and phrases are used on the video. Cross out the word or phrase that does not have a similar meaning to the word or phrase in *italics*.

1. *swift*	rapid	slow	speedy
2. *shape*	destroy	model	form
3. *commonplace*	usual	odd	ordinary
4. *aimed at*	directed toward	designed for	escaped from
5. *converging*	disconnecting	uniting	coming together
6. *device*	machine	instrument	loss
7. *limitless*	unlimited	fixed	infinite
8. *navigator*	follower	guide	pilot

9. *hint*	indication	idea	doubt
10. *zirconiums*	mineral pieces	new planets	gemstones
11. *goods*	merchandise	products	programs
12. *advocate*	supporter	opponent	promoter

IDIOMATIC EXPRESSIONS

The sentences below are from the video. What do the *italicized* expressions mean? Circle the correct answer.

1. The whole television universe is *shifting under our feet.*
   a. moving toward us
   b. changing in our own time
   c. running away from us
   d. being destroyed for us

2. There's no doubt that the future is not *just around the corner*.
   a. in the past
   b. late
   c. very near
   d. very far

3. It would take you more than 40 minutes just to *surf through* a 500-channel system.
   a. communicate with someone on
   b. disconnect all the wires in
   c. look briefly at all the channels on
   d. fit all the electric wires into

4. This is television you can really *talk back to*.
   a. communicate with in speech
   b. record the speech of
   c. imitate the speech of
   d. turn up the sound on

5. The possibility of ordering up books or health records, or receiving and sending work from the home, starts to become much more than *a pipe dream*.
   a. a practical plan
   b. a realistic goal
   c. a new invention
   d. an impossible hope

DISCUSSION

Work in groups. Discuss your answers to the following questions.

1. According to the news report, watching television is "the most commonly shared experience of American life." What is the most commonly shared experience of the people in your culture?

2. In addition to the national broadcasting systems (ABC, CBS, and NBC) and local broadcasting systems, there are a great many U.S. cable and satellite TV channels. What is the situation in the country in which you were born? Are satellite and cable TV stations common?

3. What American TV programs, if any, are you familiar with? Which ones, if any, do you like? Why?

4. Has watching this video changed or strengthened any of your ideas about the role of technology in American culture? If so, which of your ideas did it change or strengthen?

READING

Read the following excerpt from Patricia Marks Greenfield's *Mind and Media* to learn the author's view of the effects of electronic media on children. Answer the questions that follow, and then compare your answers with those of another student.

THE ELECTRONIC MEDIA

In the past few years a new medium has come along to fascinate young people and worry their elders: video games. Some adults fear that, even more than television, the games are at best frivolous and at worst mindless, numbing, and violent. While many see the popularity of microcomputers among the young as a promising trend, others fear that they reinforce asocial or even antisocial tendencies.

My own opinion is that the damaging effects the electronic media can have on children are not intrinsic to the media, but grow out of the ways the media are used. Much of the content of commercial TV shows may have a negative effect on children's social attitudes. Commercials themselves use sophisticated techniques to manipulate viewers into wanting certain products, and young children have no defenses against such techniques. And television watching <u>can</u> become a passive, deadening activity if adults do not guide their chidren's viewing and teach children to watch critically and to learn from what they watch.

But television and the newer electronic media, if used wisely, have great positive potential for learning and development. They give children different mental skills from those developed by reading and writing. Television is a better medium than the printed word for conveying certain types of information, and it makes learning available to groups of children who do not do well in traditional school situations – and even to people who cannot read. Video games introduce children to the world of microcomputers at a time when computers are becoming increasingly important both in many jobs and in daily life. The interactive quality of both video games and computers forces children actively to create stimuli and information, not merely to consume them . . .

Much has been written about the negative effects of television on children: the titles of two popular and interesting books on the subject, *The Plug-In Drug* and *Four Arguments for the Elimination of Television*, carry the message. But we do not have the option of getting rid of television. Television, video games, and other computer technology are here to stay, and their growing pervasiveness makes it all the more urgent that we discover how best to use them.

Reprinted by permission of the publishers from *Mind and Media: The Effects of Television, Video Games, and Computers*, by Patricia Marks Greenfield, Harvard University Press, Copyright© 1984 by Patricia Marks Greenfield, Cambridge Mass..

1. According to Patricia Marks Greenfield, what opinion do some adults have about video games?

_____

_____

2. Why do some adults think that the popularity of microcomputers is dangerous to young people?

_____

_____

3. In Greenfield's opinion, what is responsible for the damaging effects that the electronic media can have on children?

_____

_____

4. What does Greenfield think parents should do to prevent television watching from becoming a passive, deadening activity for their children?

_____

_____

5. According to Greenfield, what are some of the advantages of television as a medium for learning?

_____

_____

6. What positive effects of video games are mentioned in the article?

_____

_____

7. What message do the books *The Plug-In Drug* and *Four Arguments for the Elimination of Television* carry?

_____

_____

8. What is your own opinion of the effects of the electronic media (television, video games, and other computer technology) on children? Do you agree with Greenfield that these media "have great positive potential for learning and development"? Why or why not?

_____

_____

ROLE PLAY

Work in pairs. One student will play the role of the principal. The other will play the role of the head of the English department. Read the situation and the role descriptions below and decide who will play each role. After a ten-minute preparation, begin the meeting.

THE SITUATION: **A Curriculum Planning Meeting**

The principal of a high school is meeting with the head of the English department to discuss the idea of introducing more TV (news programs, documentaries, and satellite broadcasts) into the school curriculum.

ROLE DESCRIPTION: **Principal**

You are the principal of the high school. You think TV can offer great educational benefits to students. Be prepared to present your ideas for introducing more TV into the curriculum, and to respond to questions and criticism about the role of TV in schools.

ROLE DESCRIPTION: **Head of the English Department**

You are the head of the high school's English department. You think that the students already watch too much TV and that introducing more TV into the curriculum will limit students' intellectual ability. You want more stress on reading. Make up a list of questions to ask the principal about introducing more TV into the curriculum, and be prepared to criticize the idea.

WRITING

Complete one of the following activities.

1. Write a letter to media analyst Jeff Greenfield, giving your opinion of his news report on *TV Technology*.

2. Write and record a short (2–3 minutes) "broadcast" talk on how you think TV can and should be used in the classroom.

Segment 12
What's Become of Hollywood?

From: *Nightline*, 03/28/89 (edited)
Begin: 1:03:45
Length: 8:30

BEFORE YOU WATCH

TALKING POINTS

Work in groups. Discuss your answers to the following questions.

1. What was the last movie you saw on TV or at a movie theater? Was it made in Hollywood or somewhere else? How do you know?

2. Which features in the list below are typical of movies made in Hollywood? Can you think of any other typical features?

black and white	color
expensive studio sets	inexpensive studio sets
standard-size screen	wide screen
famous movie stars	unknown actors
ordinary sound	stereophonic sound
glamorous and beautiful	common and plain
fantasy	reality
low-budget productions	big-budget productions

3. Name a Hollywood star, a Hollywood director, and a Hollywood studio.

PREDICTING

Based on the title of the video segment, *What's Become of Hollywood?*, what do you think you will see and hear in the video? Write down three items under each of the headings that follow. Then compare your answers with those of another student.

SIGHTS	**WORDS**
(things you expect to see)	(words you expect to hear)

1. _____   _____

2. _____   _____

3. _____   _____

KEY WORDS

The *italicized* words in the sentences below will help you understand the video. Study the sentences. Then write your own definition for each word.

1. Before the movies became big business, people who invested in the filmmaking industry were considered to be *wildcatters*.

   wildcatters: _____

2. The actors studied the *script* until they knew their parts.

   script: _____

3. *Casablanca*, like the movie *Gone With the Wind*, is considered to be a *classic*.

   classic: _____

4. The movie was a complete *flop*; nobody who saw it enjoyed it.

   flop: _____

5. *Total Recall*, starring Arnold Schwarzenegger, was a *blockbuster*.

   blockbuster: _____

6. Many movie theaters show *trailers* of coming attractions before they present the main feature.

   trailers: _____

7. All around the city you can see *posters* advertising the latest movies.

   posters: _____

8. MGM Studios has always used a roaring lion as its *logo*.

   logo: _____

9. The producer was happy that the movie became such a great *hit*.

   hit: _____

10. Al Pacino starred in *The Godfather* and its *sequel, The Godfather II*.

    sequel: _____

WHILE YOU WATCH

GETTING THE MAIN IDEA

Watch the news report and listen for the answers to the following questions. Take brief notes on the answers. Then compare your answers with those of another student.

1:03:52– 1:12:08

What is happening to Hollywood?

Why is this happening and **how** is it affecting the movie industry?

What?	
Why?	
How?	

CHECKING YOUR PREDICTIONS

Look at the lists you made in the PREDICTING exercise on page 112. Watch the video and check (✔) the items that you actually see and hear.

1:03:52– 1:12:08

WHAT'S MISSING?

Listen to Forrest Sawyer's introduction to the news report. Fill in the missing words.

1:04:48– 1:05:38

Forrest Sawyer: Back in 1908, when a bunch of unruly (1) _____ decided to make southern California home for the unheard-of business of (2) _____ , local residents were appalled. In fact, the Hollywood Hotel stuck out a sign that read, "No (3) _____ and no (4) _____ allowed." But to everyone's amazement the wildcatters struck oil, and Hollywood was transformed from a sleepy suburb to the (5) _____ capital of the world. An industry that started out offering two features for a penny, last year took in four and a half billion dollars at the (6) _____ . It is big business now, but it's still a business for wildcatters. Only one (7) _____ in a (8) _____ is made into a movie, and only 40 percent of those movies make any profit at all. What's the movie business really like? Judd Rose begins our report with a visit to the land where dreams are high-stakes gambles.

LISTENING FOR DETAILS

1:04:48–1:10:55 Watch the video. Circle the correct answers.

1. When filmmakers moved to Hollywood in 1908, the local residents
   a. welcomed them.
   b. didn't notice them.
   c. wanted them to go away.

2. The year before this report was broadcast, the movie industry took in
   a. four and a half million dollars in ticket sales.
   b. forty-five million dollars in ticket sales.
   c. four and a half billion dollars in ticket sales.

3. Which one of the following statements is NOT true?
   a. Only one script in a thousand is made into a movie.
   b. Forty percent of all scripts become movies.
   c. Forty percent of the movies that are made make a profit.

4. The Hollywood myth was that
   a. anyone could become a movie star.
   b. you had to be rich to become a movie star.
   c. office boys and mechanics never became movie stars.

5. Which of the following statements is NOT true about *Rain Man*?
   a. It was produced by MGM studios.
   b. It's very similar to *Gone With the Wind*.
   c. It was a very successful film.

6. Who owns MGM studios now?
   a. Louis B. Mayer.
   b. Kirk Kirkorian.
   c. Ted Turner.

7. What is the total cost of producing and advertising a Hollywood film?
   a. three and a half million dollars.
   b. thirty-five million dollars.
   c. a hundred and thirty-five million dollars.

8. To break even (earn as much money as a movie costs to produce), a movie needs to earn
   a. three times its production cost.
   b. thirteen times its production cost.
   c. thirty times its production cost.

9. Why are there so many sequels among Hollywood movies?
   a. There aren't enough new scripts.
   b. They are cheap to produce.
   c. The big studios want to produce movies that are sure hits.

10. How many sequels were produced the year this report was broadcast?
    a. Three.
    b. Thirteen.
    c. Thirty.

CHECKING WHAT YOU HEAR

On the next part of the video, you will hear the names of some people, places, and movies. Who or what are they? Look at the chart below. Then watch the video as many times as you need to, and check the appropriate boxes. The first one has been done for you.

1:06:11–
1:09:10

Who or what are they?	movie	movie studio	studio owner	movie producer	movie star
Gene Kelly					✔
Esther Williams					
Lana Turner					
MGM					
Gone With the Wind					
Rain Man					
Lorimar					
Warner Brothers					
Louis B. Mayer					
Kirk Kirkorian					
Ted Turner					
Jon Peters					
Peter Guber					

NOTETAKING

Listen to the discussion about the logo for the *Batman* poster. Take brief notes on the answers to the following questions. Then compare your notes with those of another student.

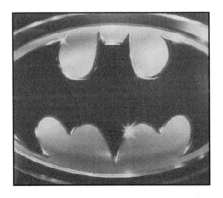

Adapted and reprinted with permission from "What's Become of Hollywood?", ABC News, *Nightline*, March 28, 1989.

1. What kind of design do the speakers want for the *Batman* poster?

   _____

   _____

2. What do they like about the *Batman* logo?

   _____

   _____

TRUE OR FALSE?

Watch the video. Are the following statements *true* or *false*? Write **T** (true) or **F** (false). Make the false statements true by changing one or two words.

1. _____ David Puttnam believes studios have been successful, but filmmakers haven't.

2. _____ Puttnam produced *Chariots of Fire*.

3. _____ Puttnam thinks that Hollywood agents aren't very powerful.

4. _____ Puttnam feels that films produced today are wonderful.

5. _____ Puttnam agreed to the salary demands of stars and their agents.

6. _____ Puttnam was president of Columbia Pictures for three years.

7. _____ There was no sequel to *Ghostbusters*.

8. _____ The message of the video is that business is more important than art in Hollywood today.

AFTER YOU WATCH

LANGUAGE POINT: CONTRASTING THE PAST AND THE PRESENT

We can use the form *used to* to indicate that something was true in the past but is not true now. Notice how the past is contrasted with the present in the following sentence:

MGM *used to be* a lion, but now it is only a kitten.

Complete the sentences below. Fill in the blanks with the correct tense of the verb in parentheses: the simple present tense or the past with *used to*.

1. Nowadays it (cost) _____ several dollars to see a movie, but it (cost) _____ only a penny to see two features.

2. People (think) _____ that anyone could become a movie star, but now they (think) _____ differently.

3. Studios (control) _____ the stars, but these days the stars (control) _____ the studios.

4. David Puttnam (be) _____ now a producer in Britain, but he (be) _____ president of Columbia Pictures.

5. Ted Turner (own) _____ MGM, but now Kirk Kirkorian (own) _____ the company.

VOCABULARY CHECK

The following excerpts are from the video. What do the *italicized* words and expressions mean? Circle the answer that is closest in meaning.

1. With the money men *calling the shots*, what's become of the movie makers of old?
   a. directing the films
   b. making the decisions
   c. making the westerns
   d. ruining the films

2. An industry that started out offering two features for a penny, last year took in $4.5 billion *at the box office*.
   a. in losses
   b. in ticket sales
   c. from films about boxing
   d. from films about business

3. The Hollywood myth was simply the American dream *draped with tinsel*.
   a. made more glamorous
   b. made less glamorous
   c. made easier
   d. made harder

4. MGM . . . now exists mainly *on paper*, run by an investment banker.
   a. in newspapers
   b. as a collection of old movie scripts
   c. as a plan for the future
   d. as a set of business contracts and financial accounts

5. MGM is now owned by a *shrewd tycoon* named Kirk Kirkorian.
   a. rich person with no business experience
   b. clever person who has become rich and successful in business
   c. poor person with a lot of business experience
   d. stupid person who has become rich and successful in business

6. So Peters and Guber are *keeping a close eye on* everything, from the trailers to the posters.
   a. looking carefully at
   b. shutting their eyes at
   c. discovering
   d. stopping people from seeing

DISCUSSION

Work in pairs. Discuss your answers to the following questions.

1. How many movies have you seen in the past year?
2. How many were American? How many were from foreign films?
3. What are three of your favorite movies?
4. What kinds of movies do you like best? action thrillers? comedies? romances? musicals? dramas? cartoons?
5. Do you agree that movies are not as good as they used to be? Why or why not?

ROLE PLAY

Work in pairs. One student will play the role of the interviewer. The other will play the role of the producer. Read the situation and the role descriptions below and decide who will play each role. After a ten-minute preparation, begin the interview.

THE SITUATION: **A Radio Interview**

A radio program called "Movie Talk" has invited a Hollywood producer to talk about Judd Rose's ABC news report, *What's Become of Hollywood?* and the future of filmmaking.

ROLE DESCRIPTION: **Interviewer**

You are the interviewer for "Movie Talk". Prepare a list of questions to ask the producer. Base your questions on Judd Rose's ABC news report *What's Become of Hollywood?*

You are a successful Hollywood producer. You have seen the
report *What's Become of Hollywood?* Be prepared to answer any
critical questions the interviewer might ask.

READING

Later in the program, Forrest Sawyer interviewed film star Kirk Douglas.
and asked him, "Is it easier to make a career in movies now than it was
when you started?" Read Kirk Douglas' reply. Then use the information in
his reply to complete the chart that follows.

WHO IS OSCAR?

Oscar is the name of the most famous movie award in the world. The Oscar Awards ceremonies are seen on TV by 96 million people around the world, double the number of actual moviegoers. It is the one of the most successful advertising gimmicks in the world. But it began as a way of fighting the movie industry unions in Hollywood.

Oscar is thirteen and a half inches tall, weighs eight and a half pounds, and costs just over $100 to make. It was designed by a committee chairman in 1926. The film star Bette Davis claimed it was named after her husband at that time, Harmon Oscar Nelson. Not everyone agrees with her.

Oscars are voted for by the 5,000 plus members of the Academy of Motion Picture Arts and Sciences, based in Los Angeles. To be eligible for an Oscar a movie must be shown in a Los Angeles movie theater for at least a week before New Year's Eve of the previous year. Ballot papers for the election are distributed in January, and nominations are announced in mid-February. On Oscar night in March, after weeks of parties and other awards, everyone gathers in Los Angeles for the ceremony. No one knows in advance who the winners will be. The votes are counted and guarded by the accounting firm, Price Waterhouse until the night of the Oscars.

You wouldn't think that all this activity started as an attempt to beat the unions. In 1926 Louis B. Mayer, the head of Metro-Goldwyn-Mayer Studios, found that movie production costs were rising because of the Basic Studio Agreement, a contract between Hollywood studios and labor unions. Many Hollywood actors were joining labor unions. To stop this, Mayer proposed an alternative to the unions: the Academy of Motion Pictures Arts and Sciences. He invited leading film actors, producers, and directors to join this new, prestigious organization. The first meeting took place in 1927, and the Academy Awards, a complete afterthought, were first presented in 1929. Those early members of the Academy did not know that the Oscars would become the most important part of the Academy's work.

1. What is seen by 96 million people?

   _____

2. What costs $100?

   _____

3. How many members of the Academy of Motion Picture Arts and Sciences are there?

   _____

4. When is Oscar night?

   _____

5. Who was Louis B. Mayer?

   _____

6. When were the first awards?

   _____

7. When was the Academy founded?

   _____

WRITING

Complete one of the following activities.

1. Write a 150 word movie review for your local paper or school magazine. Describe a movie you have recently seen in a movie theater or on TV.
2. What's wrong with Hollywood? Write a letter to Kirk Kirkorian. Describe what kinds of films you want to see and what you don't want to see on the movie screen.

Steven Briganti, Ellis Island Restorer

from *World News Tonight*, September 7, 1990

Announcer: From ABC this is *World News Tonight* with Peter Jennings.

Peter Jennings: Finally this evening, our Person of the Week. There has been a great deal of attention paid this week to all of the refugees created by the situation in Iraq and Kuwait. Hundreds of thousands of people fleeing because they are suddenly no longer able to make a living, even worse, fearing that they may be trapped in the middle of a war — which reminded us that this weekend millions of Americans will have an opportunity to contemplate the refugees in their past.

Steven Briganti: Well, I'm a firm believer that we can't know how we are as people or as a nation unless we know where we came from - and how we got here.

Peter Jennings: Steven Briganti is responsible for making sure we know. Briganti is the guiding force at the foundation that has renovated and restored the Ellis Island Immigration Center in the port of New York. This weekend it will be rededicated as the Ellis Island Immigration Museum, a monument to the greatest migration of human beings in modern history.

Professor David Reimers, Historian: There's a little bit of romance about Ellis Island today, I think. It used to have that reputation of the place of tears or because it was going to reject people and their anxiety. We tend to forget some of those things.

Peter Jennings: Briganti's own family came through here from Italy.

Steven Briganti: I had a deep feeling for Ellis Island in particular. Three of my four grandparents came through here. My mother came through.

Peter Jennings: Briganti was born in New York City and raised in Indiana. He studied history at Butler University.

Steven Briganti: I heard a lot of stories about Ellis Island from my mother who'd come through, but as a child I didn't pay too much attention to it.

Peter Jennings: It was in 1892, when the Great Immigration Hall at Ellis Island first opened. By the end of World War II in 1945, 17 million people would sail through New York's gateway to the rest of America. They came mostly from Europe. They came to escape oppression and hunger at home.

Steven Briganti: I think they were brave pioneers who were looking for more opportunity or running away from tyranny.

Peter Jennings: Through the late 1920s, 5,000 people a day were herded in and processed in Ellis Island's Great Hall. It was at Ellis Island where it was decided if you could stay in America. Welcome or not, it was often a frightening experience.

Steven Briganti: And suddenly here they were in the Great Hall, all 5,000 a day, all different languages, a lot of noise, a lot of confusion, but nevertheless, perhaps the greatest moment of their lives.

Peter Jennings: Bertha Devlin came from Ireland in 1923. She was 22 then.

Bertha Devlin: The place was packed. There was no room to move around — every kind of people, every nationality.

Peter Jennings: By the 1950s, the great wave of European immigration to America had subsided. Ellis Island was closed. In the three decades since, it went very much to seed.

Steven Briganti: Isn't it amazing that in 1954 when this building closed down, even though 40 percent of the population of the country had come through it, we didn't know what to do with it. So, we abandoned it.

Peter Jennings: Until 1984 when Briganti and the Ellis Island Foundation began to raise money. Briganti then began marshaling the architects and the construction crews. His idea was to preserve the memories of Ellis Island, both good and bad. Like the infamous stairway which new immigrants took to have their medical exam. The doctors watched as people climbed. If a limp was evident or shortness of breath was detected, they were marked with an "X" and very often deported. Steven Briganti is very pleased with the way the restoration has turned out. Americans may now come here for the first time or some of them can come again to think about their nation's past and perhaps find inspiration for the future.

Steven Briganti: People were coming here looking for new opportunity, looking for a new way of life. They came at the turn of the century. They continue to come today looking for new hope, for new opportunities, and that's what Ellis Island is symbolic of.

Peter Jennings: And so we choose Steven Briganti. Before he became the guardian of this Ellis Island project, he was in charge of refurbishing the Statue of Liberty. We choose him because of what he's done to help us all further appreciate two of the basic values for which America stands: liberty and sanctuary.

Announcer: This has been a presentation of ABC News. Where more Americans get their news than from any other source.

TRANSCRIPT 2

Spike Lee on His Movie, *Do the Right Thing*
from *World News Tonight*, July 7, 1989

Announcer: From ABC this is *World News Tonight* with Peter Jennings.

Peter Jennings: Finally this evening, our Person of the Week. So many people are talking about him this week. The film which he produced and directed and wrote and starred in has just opened at movie houses all across the country, and all the attention can't hurt at the box office. But he will be particularly pleased because he's made an unusual film, a controversial film, one which may make a difference.

Spike Lee: My job as a filmmaker, I feel, is to present the problems. Put it out there. I think that because of this film, I think that a lot more people will be talking about race relations today in this country.

Peter Jennings: There is no doubt about that. Spike Lee's film, *Do the Right Thing* touches all sorts of nerves. [**Crew member:** Alright. Quiet for rehearsal. Camera ready.] The film deals with life in the New York City neighborhood of Bedford Stuyvesant. Throughout one long hot day there is a series of incidents between blacks and the white characters in the film: Sal, who built and owns Sal's Pizzeria, who has done business quite contentedly here for 25 years, and his two sons, one of whom can hardly wait to escape what he regards as a totally hostile environment.

Son (movie scene) to Sal: *I'm sick of niggers. It's like I come to work, it's Planet of the Apes. I don't like being around them. They're animals.*

Sal/Danny Aiello: *Why you got so much anger in you?*

Peter Jennings: There's anger among blacks as well. As when a young white man accidentally wheels his bicycle over the brand new sneaker of the neighborhood's most provocative troublemaker who goes by the name of "Buggin' Out."

Buggin' Out (movie scene): *Who told you to walk on my side of the block? Who told you to be in my neighborhood?*

Man/John Savage: *I own this brownstone.*

Buggin' Out: *Who told you to buy a brownstone on my block, in my neighborhood, on my side of the street?*

Peter Jennings: Buggin' Out tries to organize a black boycott of the pizzeria because Sal only has pictures of famous Italians on his "Wall of Fame." [**Buggin' Out:** *Hey Sal, how come you got no brothers on the wall here?* **Sal:** *You want brothers on the wall. Get your own place. You can do what you wanna do.*] The film makes the point that there is a measure of racism in everyone.

Spike Lee: I mean, this movie is not science fiction, it's not Walt Disney and it's not E.T. It's the state of race relations today in America.

Peter Jennings: Or at least Spike Lee's view of race relations. Spike Lee was born in Atlanta and grew up in a middle class family in Brooklyn. Spike Lee is 32, "only 32" to some of his critics who find his portrayal of both the neighborhood and its characters in this film unsophisticated and immature.

Stanley Crouch, Writer: Do we have to discuss racism on an MTV level of intellectual depth, which is what Spike Lee represents?

Peter Jennings: For the *Newsweek* critic, David Ansen, it is the most informed view of racism that an American filmmaker has ever delivered.

David Ansen: He doesn't want to let anybody off the hook too easily. I think he's trying to prick consciences and get people talking.

Spike Lee: Because in America the same value is not put on a black life as it is on a white life. A white life. Just look at the reviews of this film. A lot of these people, all they do is harp upon the destruction of Sal's Pizzeria, never once mentioning the police murdering of Radio Raheem in the film.

Peter Jennings: The total breakdown of any understanding comes when Radio Raheem, very much the block's bully, refuses to turn down his boom box in the pizzeria. [**Radio Raheem:** *Two slices.* **Sal:** *Turn it off.* **Male:** *It's the Radio Raheem.* **Sal:** *I can't even hear myself think.*] Sal loses his cool, destroys the radio, calling his abusers by the dreaded word "nigger" and all hell breaks loose. The cops come, and one of them, perhaps his own racism having taken over, kills Radio Raheem. In no time, racism replaces reason altogether.

Dr. Alvin Poussaint, Harvard University: He spares no one in really trying to delve in and examine what's going on in their psyches that lead to these kinds of conflicts that can end in riots and the destruction of communities and ultimately perhaps of society.

Peter Jennings: Lee is criticized by those who believe he has thoughtlessly or calculatingly risked inciting real violence. What Lee says he wants to ignite is debate.

Spike Lee: The state of race relations today in America is not a fairy tale. It has never been a fairy tale. Despite what people want to keep believing, *Do the Right Thing* is asking one simple question: "Can we, and are we, going to live together?"

Peter Jennings: And so we choose Spike Lee, whose film has prompted us to think about the great black American poet, the late Langston Hughes, who wondered in one poem, "What happens to a dream deferred? Does it dry up like a raisin in the sun, or fester like a sore?" Maybe, Hughes wrote,"It just sags like a heavy load. Or does it explode?" That's our report on *World News Tonight*.

Announcer: This has been a presentation of ABC News. Where more Americans get their news than from any other source.

TRANSCRIPT 3

Those Terrible Taxis!
from *20/20*, March 30, 1990

Announcer 1: From ABC News. Around the world and into your home, the stories that touch your life, with Hugh Downs and Barbara Walters. This is *20/20* tonight.

Announcer 2: New York cabbies - the drivers everyone loves to hate.

Female: I've had him slam the door in my face. Drive away while I was half in the car.

Announcer 1: John Stossel asks, "Is it true what they say about those terrible taxis?"

Barbara Walters: There was a story in the newspaper a few weeks ago about a New York taxi driver who was, they say, ripped off an unsuspecting tourist. He hit him for $15 for a fare that should have cost, a couple of dollars, at best.

Well, that may fit your view of New York cab drivers in general and that's why we asked John Stossel to give us a sense of the world of New York cab drivers.

John Stossel: Okay. You've made it to Kennedy Airport. You've survived the flight, but now you've really got something to worry about: the New York taxi driver. You've heard the stories; they're rude, reckless. These are tough native New Yorkers who know all the tricks. They'll cheat you on the fare, maybe drop you off at some hellhole miles away from your hotel. Well, some of the stories are true. What you might not know is that when cab drivers live up to the vicious stereotype, we customers can file a complaint that'll force them to come here.

Taxi Court Clerk: Give me your name, time, and your hack number.

1st Passenger: He also refused to let us out of the cab.

Mary, Passenger: I mean, isn't there an abduction rule or could you start one for this guy?

1st Taxi Driver: You want to get nasty with me? You're gonna have a real problem.

John Stossel: This nasty-sounding place is called Taxi Court.

Brian J. Burstin, Administrative Law Judge: With regard to the Driver's Rule 203a, which is "The driver shall be courteous to passengers," it's quite clear that didn't occur here.

2nd Judge: How do you plead? Guilty or not guilty?

2nd Taxi Driver: But I don't remember what—

John Stossel: Lots of people here complain about taxis not picking them up.

Tyrone Rice, Passenger: I opened the door, they almost shot me.

John Stossel: Tyrone Rice says this driver stopped, looked Rice over and then drove on.

Tyrone Rice: And I'm tired of getting refused. I think it's because they're scared a driver's going to rob them or whatever.

Mary: They won't take me—failure to take me to my destination happens so many times 'cause they just don't feel like it. They don't feel like it and they're not going.

Morty Krauss, Taxi Driver: Last year, twenty-six cab drivers were killed in this city. There's reasons why drivers refuse to go to certain areas.

John Stossel: There's always another side to the story. Let's look at it from the driver's point of view. They know their reputation. You cab drivers are rude, you cheat people.

3rd Taxi Driver: Everybody tries to nice. Everybody tries to nice.

4th Taxi Driver: I am driving this cab from two years. I never cheat anybody.

John Stossel: Whether you believe them or not, your ears should tell you that one part of the stereotype isn't true. These are not tough native New Yorkers. Where are you from?

Hernando Cuervo, Taxi Driver: Well, I'm originally from Colombia.

4th Taxi Driver: I'm from India, sir.

5th Taxi Driver: Middle East.

3rd Taxi Driver: I'm from Pakistan.

John Stossel: Today, nearly every driver is an immigrant. We natives don't want the job 'cause it's too hard, too hard to make money because the city's licensing bureau has set up a little cartel. You may own a yellow cab only if you have a medallion. You can only get a medallion by buying one from a company that already owns one. The cost: $130,000. As a result, new drivers rent cabs from medallion owners for $80 a day. That's why the cabbie's always pushing, always in a rush. If he doesn't get enough fares, he could drive all day and lose money. It's such a grind that today most drivers quit after just four and half months. Or sometimes, they'll just get mad and end up in taxi court.

Lester Margolis, Taxi Driver: With every move that I was making, they were shouting to make a left, make a right, slow down, and so on and so forth.

John Stossel: Some drivers say this is a class issue. Passengers don't respect the driver.

Lester Margolis: I recall your boyfriend insulting me. I recall him saying that I was never going to be anything more than a taxicab driver.

John Stossel: Do some passengers have an attitude?

Hernando Cuervo: Yes. Some passengers think that they're better than you in a certain way where they think that you're not educated.

Pierre Jacquet Reynould, Taxi Driver: I'm from Haiti. I speak three languages. I speak English, French and Spanish, with writing and everything.

John Stossel: Many drivers are more educated than their passengers, and passengers might also be surprised to learn that each driver, before he's even allowed to drive, must pay $150 to take a 40-hour course where he'll be taught things like "proper demeanor."

Taxi School Instructor: Now, if you respect the passenger, you're courteous, what are they going to respond back to you with?

1st Student: A tip.

2nd Student: A good tip.

Instructor: A good tip and what? Respect.

John Stossel: They prepare for rude passengers by playing roles.

3rd Student: Take me to Jersey City now! I'm in a hurry.

4th Student: Good morning, sir.

John Stossel: You're supposed to be nice, even if the passenger isn't.

3rd Student: New Jersey? You ever heard of New Jersey?

4th Student: I heard about it, sir.

John Stossel: Watching these students beginning a new life, eager to make it in

America, gives you a different perspective on the cab driver stereotype. Here, the more experienced immigrants help the others. Of course, no class is complete without the field trip.

Bus Guide: If you look to the right now, you'll see that Fifth Avenue is right down the end. We'll be passing that a little bit later. Even streets go east. Right, odd streets go west.

John Stossel: In one long day, he must learn the quirks of the city, the worst traffic, all the one-way streets.

Guide: Now, look at this intersection. Right underneath it, what does it say? Waverly and Waverly. This is the only street in Manhattan that crosses itself.

John Stossel: This is confusing even to natives.

Guide: On the left, we have what? Carnegie Hall. Now, how do we get there? How do we get to Carnegie Hall? By practicing.

John Stossel: American jokes go right by this group. There's too much to learn because this is the opportunity to fulfill the dream: financial independence in America. For those who pass the licensing test, the dream will live for a few more months. Then reality will interfere.

Ioan Gheorghe, Taxi Driver: You get shot or you get killed anytime.

6th Taxi Driver: Anytime.

Ioan Gheorghe: Doesn't matter if it's daytime or if it's nighttime.

John Stossel: So why are you driving a cab?

Ioan Gheorghe: Because I have no choice. I am an immigrant.

John Stossel: Where are you from?

Ioan Gheorghe: I am from Romania.

John Stossel: And this gave you freedom, a chance to make some money?

Ioan Gheorghe: Yeah, that's it, to make some living. Nothing else, a living.

John Stossel: You know, Hugh, I've lived here 15 years and I must have taken a thousand cabs. I don't know about you, but I've never really had a bad experience.

Hugh Downs: No, most of them are decent. I met one once that was so secure that I didn't have money with me and he said, "That's all right." He said, "Mail it to me," and he gave me a card.

John Stossel: But he recognized you.

Hugh Downs: No, I don't think he did. I really don't think he did. And we corresponded later and he said he had never been burned by doing that, so there was a philosopher cab driver. Thank you, John. And that's 20/20 for tonight. We thank you for being with us.

Barbara Walters: And remember, we're in touch, so you be in touch. I'm Barbara Walters.

Hugh Downs: And I'm Hugh Downs.

Barbara Walters: And from all of us here at *20/20* have a good weekend and good night.

TRANSCRIPT 4

Maya Angelou, Inaugural Poetess

from *World News Tonight*, January 22, 1993

Narrator: From ABC this is *World News Tonight* with Peter Jennings.

Peter Jennings: Finally this evening, our Person of the Week, by way of reminder, really, because it's unlikely that you missed her this week. The day before yesterday, this woman was given an uncommon opportunity to have an influence on a vast audience of people. And to paraphrase her message then, she certainly seized the moment.

Maya Angelou: I really try to get into the content of the poem and then I suspend myself. You see, it's not that I suspend all disbelief and belief, I suspend myself.

[Reading Poem] *Across the wall of the world, a river sings a beautiful song. It says, "Come. Rest here by my side."*

Peter Jennings: Maya Angelou made it clear that Bill Clinton's inauguration would be different. No poet had been engaged for such an occasion in 32 years and very few poets have ever engaged such an audience as did she.

Maya Angelou: [Reading] *The Catholic, the Muslim, the French, the Greek, the Irish, the rabbi, the priest, the sheik, the gay, the straight, the preacher, the privileged, the homeless, the teacher: they all hear the speaking of the tree.*

I wanted to say that despite our differences in color and shape, and sizes and privilege, and even postures, that we are more alike than we are unalike.

Peter Jennings: Maya Angelou has sung and danced, acted and taught, written and recited for 40 years. "I speak to the black experience," she says, "but I am always talking about the human condition."

Maya Angelou: [Reading] *Someone was lonely before you, frightened before you, humiliated before you, neglected before you, beaten before you, raped before you. And yet, someone has survived. My God.*

Peter Jennings: In her autobiography, *I Know Why the Caged Bird Sings*, Angelou describes life growing up in the segregated South. Stamps, Arkansas is not far from Hope, from whence comes the president. She went back for the first time as an adult.

Maya Angelou: I was terribly hurt in this town and vastly loved.

Peter Jennings: We know now that Maya was raised by her grandmother and uncle in the back of this store. The only black store in Stamps. She was raped when she was seven.

Maya Angelou: For 5 and a half years, I refused to speak. I had voice, but I refused to use it.

128

Peter Jennings: Instead, she developed her imagination.

Maya Angelou: This store was my favorite place to be. Alone and empty in the morning, it looked like an unopened present from a stranger. Opening the front doors was pulling the ribbon off the unexpected gift. At 12 and a half, I returned to my voice. I decided I would render Portia's speech from *The Merchant of Venice* in the Seamee Church. That's right. It was going to knock them off those pews.

Peter Jennings: As she did this week from the steps of the nation's capitol.

Maya Angelou: [Reading poem] *Lift up your faces. You have a piercing need for this bright morning dawning for you. History, despite its wrenching pain, cannot be unlived, but if faced with courage, need not be lived again.*

We have a history that is loaded with cruelty and with glory. And we have to see that. If we don't admit that, we have no chance of building a tomorrow for our children.

Peter Jennings: And so she urged the new president and the new faces in the crowd, the seen and the unseen, "seize the moment."

Maya Angelou: [Reading poem] *Here, on the pulse of this new day, you may have the grace to look up and out and into your sister's eyes and into your brother's face, your country, and say simply, very simply, with hope, "Good morning."*

Peter Jennings: And so we choose Maya Angelou. It isn't often the case that an American poet gets such a public opportunity to perform. It's quite different in some other countries. In Russia, for example, it is not uncommon for 20,000 people to show up just to hear a poet. This week, at least, Ms. Angelou was heard by millions. That's our report on World News Tonight; *20/20* later. Have a good weekend. We'll see you on Monday. Good night.

Announcer: This has been a presentation of ABC News. More Americans get their news from ABC News than from any other source.

TRANSCRIPT 5

Paul Simon

from *World News Tonight*, October 22, 1993

Announcer: From ABC , this is *World News Tonight* with Peter Jennings.

Peter Jennings: Finally, this evening, our Person of the Week — someone very familiar. A man who has certainly endured and who manages after, lo, these many years to remind more than one generation that talent is a gift and sharing that gift has made a great deal of difference to a great many people. We choose him this week because we're at that age to be nostalgic and because he keeps moving his art forward.

Paul Simon: Well, I became — I became fascinated with making records and writing songs from the age of 13. I never lost my interest.

Peter Jennings: Paul Simon, the songwriter-singer who turned 52 last week, has no intention of slip-sliding away to anywhere. He has just released the collected works of 30 years and this week he is performing in a sold-out, 21-show retrospective concert, *Back Together Again*, with his former partner, Art Garfunkel. There is such a timely quality about Paul Simon's lyrics.

Jon Pareles, New York Times Music Critic: He manages to focus things clearly. He manages to have a line or a phrase or a couplet or a verse that just says this is how things are now. This is the way the world is now. And he can do that and he can make it stick in your head.

Peter Jennings: They were two childhood friends from New York City, Paul and Art Garfunkel. "The Sounds of Silence" was a huge hit for them in 1965.

[Film clip from *The Graduate*]

Dustin Hoffman: *Mrs Robinson, you're trying to seduce me.*

Peter Jennings: Simon wrote the music and lyrics for *The Graduate* in 1967, including the song, "Mrs. Robinson." For many, the song signified the country's loss of innocence and the dearth of heroes for a generation in rebellion against an unpopular war. Then came, "A Bridge Over Troubled Water." 10 million copies it sold. Maybe it signified Simon and Garfunkel's own troubles.

Paul Simon: I probably had begun that separation during the making of "Bridge Over Troubled Water." So we were just in very different places, musically.

Peter Jennings: They broke up a year later. It was in the 70s that Simon began to incorporate the music and other influences of other cultures , that would mold his social message as a single performer. He took a lot of heat for going to South Africa. He was accused of breaking the economic boycott and exploiting South African black performers, though they didn't all seem to think so. And *Graceland* was an enormously successful album. It introduced Ladysmith Black Mambazo to a much wider world. On *Rhythm of the Saints*, Simon incorporated the culture of Brazil. It made for a powerful international blend, with African and American influence. Simon and Garfunkel together have always been a nostalgic draw — 1981 in Central Park, and again today. Whatever they think of each other, the public will always pay to see them. But it is Paul Simon who's always made such a difference to American music, who has always gone on to greater heights.

Paul Simon: What I think to myself is "Don't think about what you're going to do in your profession. Think about what it is that you want to do with music."

Peter Jennings: And so we choose Paul Simon, who has done so much with music, who's led him and us on a very interesting voyage through our own times. Pretty fast to be going through his history, but there you are. That's our report on *World New Tonight*. I'm Peter Jennings. Don't forget *20/20* later. Have a good weekend. Good night.

Announcer: This has been a presentation of ABC News. More Americans get their news from ABC News than from any other source.

Poetry in America

from *Nightline*, June 18, 1992

Poet 1: *As though it were reluctant to be day*
Morning deploys a scale of rarities and gray.

Poet 2: *Turn around*
Run it home backwards - stop
Wrap her lips 'round midnight nice and ...

Poet 3: *It is hot today, dry enough for cutting grain*
And I am drifting back to North Dakota where butterflies are all
gone brown

Poet 4: *Homage to my hips*
These hips are big hips
They need space to move around

Poet 5 (Rap):
This is poetry in the form of street talk
Scorpio from DC
And I'll be loud in New York

Poet 6: *This is the story of the unknown soldier.*
He was the first to land, the last to leave with his own hand.

Ted Koppel: Tonight we address the question, "Who cares about poetry in America?"

Announcer: This is ABC News *Nightline*. Reporting from Washington, Ted Koppel.

Ted Koppel: When I was a child, growing up in England, parents – not just mine, but almost all parents—placed enormous stock in the health-giving power of cod liver oil. Despite the fact that I was repeatedly told how good it was for me, I learned to loathe cod liver oil.

Unfortunately, some parents and many teachers dispense poetry the same way. We would like, if humanly possible, to undo some of that damage tonight. Indeed, perhaps a warning is in order. Poetry has the power to arouse and inflame, to evoke the most private of emotions. It can be polemical or funny, it can rhyme, but it doesn't have to, and there is some danger that you may enjoy it.

Six men and women will be joining us tonight to perform some poetry, most of it, their own. But first, my colleague Dave Marash will introduce you to the startling proposition that poetry can be popular.

Bob Holman: All right! Poetry lives. Crack those ears! Here we go!

1st Reader: *To the third-rate poet who drifted off into eternal obscurity, teasing and tempting Kismet by screaming, "I just want to say something."*

2nd Reader: *Why didn't you run to me first? I'm the female warrior, you know, perfectly willing to melt down my armor.*

Bob Holman, Nuyorican Poets' Cafe: What's going on here is a mix of people and types, all centered around words that you can dance to.

Dave Marash: Words shimmy and slam out of MC Bob Holman's mouth as he launches another set of improvised poetry at New York's Nuyorican Poets' Cafe. Rap, Holman says, has people listening to lyrics again. Miguel Algarin, the poet/scholar who helped found the cafe, thinks it's a combination of early 60's literary energy and early 90s economics that's made the cafe a popular place for low-cost weekend dates.

Miguel Algarin: It's clear that this new game, tongue-in-cheek thing that we have going called "The Poetry Slam" has made it a fun, popular place to come to hear poetry on a Friday night when you would ordinarily want to go out dancing.

3rd Reader: *Didn't I make myself clear? My paradise is lost, but I don't want the crack poison out of control, I want the New York extra-sharp cheddar, cheddar, cheddar, yeah, that's all I want!* Thanks.

Miguel Algarin: Who comes? I think everybody comes. It's definitely young, and it's definitely alive.

Dave Marash: The oral improvised poetry of the Nuyorican Poets' Cafe lives for the moment, in the open air. But the more enduring poetry read by the crowd who came to welcome poet laureate Joseph Brodsky to the Library of Congress last September, can live on only on paper. And poetry in print, Brodsky told his admirers, isn't reaching enough people.

Joseph Brodsky: I don't rightly know what's worse, burning books or not reading them.

Dave Marash: How to get more people reading poetry? Brodsky's answer is simple: print more poetry, and put it before more people.

Joseph Brodsky: You can publish an anthology of American poetry and put it in a drawer of every motel in this country. The Bible won't object. The Bible doesn't object to the phone book next to it.

Dave Marash: If Brodsky has his way, you'll find poetry in hotel rooms, on newsstands, even in supermarkets. Brodsky says he's already had a letter from the *National Enquirer* offering to print American poetry, but he wants more. He wants whole books of poems racked right here, you know, *The Globe, The Enquirer, The Star, The Examiner*, and Emily Dickinson.

Leon Wieseltier, *The New Republic*: Well, maybe the person who buys the *Enquirer* won't want to buy Emily Dickinson, but maybe her boyfriend will, and maybe his kid will.

Dave Marash: Some literary people think Brodsky's on to something. Some don't.

Jane Friedman, Knopf Books: I wish I could say that it was a possible dream. I think it is an impossible dream. Just to down-market a book because it is a good book and you want to reach the broadest possible audience, I'm afraid, is not a reality today.

Dave Marash: Reality, for Jane Friedman, is her recently revived *Everyman's*

Library. Great books, but at a $15 to $22 price, a far cry from Brodsky's books for a buck or two.

Richard Wilbur: This comes out of my first meeting with Joseph Brodsky.
A thrush, because I'd been wrong,
Burst rightly into song,
In a world not vague, not lonely,
Not governed by me only.

Dave Marash: Former poet laureate Richard Wilbur agrees with his friend Brodsky.

Richard Wilbur: I think that books of poetry are frighteningly priced at present.

Dave Marash: Wilbur and another former laureate, Mark Strand, disagree that mass marketing can create a massive audience for poetry.

Mark Strand, FMR Poet Laureat: There has to be a way in which poetry is made not only available, but made necessary. And just because it appears on supermarket shelves doesn't mean that people are going to find it a need. And I think they're gonna have to be educated to feel that poetry or, in fact, any other writing that is demanding is necessary.

Ntozake Shange, Poet & Playwright: This is supposed to make art accessible and easily available to everybody, like corn and potatoes.

Dave Marash: Poet and playwright Ntozake Shange has found it easy to communicate the necessity of literary art. She and several other famous writers are part of a program called The "Writers' Voice", launched in Manhattan to put together published and unpublished authors from Maine to Montana.

Ntozake Shange: I got to Billings, and I couldn't believe it was so small. People in the hotel, people in the street, I went to a bakery, they were all getting ready to come to this big—the biggest hall in the town to see two poets, Maxine Kumin and myself .

Dave Marash: Another "Writer's Voice" participant says, "Great poets at the town hall makes the same kind of good sense as poetry at the mall or market."

Roy Blount, Jr., Writer: People can be reached on a—you know, engaged in a serious way without necessarily being engaged in a high-toned sort of preconceivedly literary way. I think that the best writers have always—well, the greatest writers have always written for big audiences.

Joseph Brodsky: We are all literate, therefore everybody is a potential reader of poetry. It is on this assumption that the distribution of books should be based.

Bob Holman: Poetry can be a dense form of language and can need a guide or a machete to get through the thickets to meaning. That's fine, that can be a wonderful experience. It takes a kind of tuning up of the eyes and the ears to be able to do that. Maybe for that kind of poetry you need a college education. But that's not the only kind of poetry that there is.

Dave Marash: Poetry, plain or not-so-simple, doesn't lack for advocates or, it would seem, makers or consumers. A good thing, too, because for as Roy

Blount, Jr. reminds us, "We need language that's honest and strong to have an America that's honest and strong." Or, to put into the kind of pop lyrics that Bob Holman might dance to," America, the song is you". I'm Dave Marash for *Nightline*, in Washington.

Ted Koppel: That's our report for tonight. I'm Ted Koppel in Washington. For all of us here at ABC News, good night.

Announcer: *Nightline* is a presentation of ABC News. More Americans get their news from ABC News than from any other source.

TRANSCRIPT 7

Why Girls Lose Self-Confidence in Their Teens
from *World News Tonight*, April 27, 1993

Announcer: From ABC this is *World News Tonight* with Peter Jennings

Peter Jennings: Finally, this evening, on the *American Agenda*, our daughters. Tomorrow at many companies around the country, parents are going to take their daughters to work. It's the idea of a women's organization called the "Ms. Foundation," and the point is to show girls their future value in the workplace to help convince them that they are taken seriously. Our Agenda reporter, Carole Simpson, on why girls, in particular, need such a message.

Carole Simpson: Teenage girls closed their eyes and tried to imagine themselves as boys.

High School Teacher: If you were a boy, okay, would they expect you to do different things around the house, or nothing at all around the house?

Carole Simpson: An English teacher at New York City's Humanities High School conducts the experiment.

High School Teacher: So let's get back into your own bodies.

Carole Simpson: The girls are asked if they would prefer to have been born male. These were typical answers.

Samantha Radcliffe, Age 16: Yeah, I do want to… I'd rather be a man because they definitely have power, and that's just the way it is.

Quiana Hilton, Age15: If I could be a man today, I would, because men get everything they want the easy way.

Carole Simpson: Research shows that until nine or ten, these girls probably didn't think this way.

Marie Wilson, "Ms. Foundation" President: I think we forget that because daughters are anchored in powerful relationships with us and with other… with a woman's world, almost, in school, they start off powerfully and they feel powerful. I mean, that's why they have a sense of self-esteem.

Carole Simpson: What happens? This is what happens.

(TV Commercial): *Shake that body.*

(TV Commercial): *Your body, trim - fit.*

Heather Silver, Age 17: You never hear the guys saying, "Oh, my God, I have to lose ten pounds. I'm so fat."

3rd Actor: Hey, hey lady.

4th Actor: Lashes that get noticed.

Sheila Keane, Age 17: This is what the guys look at. This is what beauty is.

Lyn Mikel Brown, Colby College: They begin to get messages about how to be in the world if they're going to be accepted as women; about how to feel, what to say, what to think, and they start to struggle with that.

Carole Simpson: In a five-year study of girls' psychological development, Lyn Mikel Brown and Harvard's Carol Gilligan found that girls lose self-esteem during adolescence. As they mature sexually, the researchers say, they begin to get the message that the ideal woman is meant to be seen more than heard. At Washington, DC's Georgetown Day Middle School, we made our own comparison of younger and adolescent girls. The fourth grade girls were self-assured and outspoken.

Joy Burgess, Age 9: I have the freedom of doing what I want to do. Nobody can … almost nobody can make me do what I don't want to do.

Lee McClain, Age 9: I get really aggravated when people tell me that I can't do something.

Carole Simpson: But here, as in classrooms across America, girls begin to feel minimized by textbooks and by teachers who still call on them less frequently than boys; a phenomenon documented by a recent study by the American Association of University Women. When we talked to eighth-grade girls at Georgetown Day, we could see the loss of self-esteem inside and outside the classroom.

Dawn Mason, Age 13: There's this voice in my head telling me, "You know the answer and you can verbalize it well and you know you can do it," and then there's this other voice saying, "Well, it's not going to come out right and it's not going to sound as good as what someone else has said."

Mercy Horst, Age 13: You feel like you have to be a certain way in order for them to like you.

Carole Simpson: Experts say the fear of not living up to unrealistic expectations is to blame for the high rate of teenage pregnancies and the growing number of girls who suffer eating disorders, depression, and suicidal tendencies. They increasingly believe that the key to building a girl's confidence is her mother. Hila Richardson is the mother of a typical nine-year-old girl, full of spunk.

Rebecca Klasfeld, Age 9: I horseback ride. I do push-ups almost every day. I'm stronger than some of the boys in my classes.

Carole Simpson: Rebecca's mom is struggling not to teach her daughter what she and most women say they learned from their mothers: that girls have to be nice and pretty and quiet. Instead, Hila is teaching Rebecca to be herself.

Hila Richardson: I hope I give her messages of how much she's valued and how important she's been in my life.

Marie Wilson: Let's teach our daughters confidence. Let's start focusing on what our daughters can do, you know, not who they can look like … but what they can do in the world.

Carole Simpson: Carole Simpson, ABC News, New York.

Peter Jennings: That's our report on *World News Tonight*. *NightLine* later. I'm Peter Jennings. Good night.

Announcer: This has been a presentation of ABC News. More Americans get their news from ABC News than from any other source.

TRANSCRIPT 8

Hillary Rodham Clinton
from *World News Tonight*, September 24, 1993

Announcer: From ABC this is World News Tonight with Peter Jennings.

Peter Jennings: Finally this evening, our Person of the Week. It is one of the more obvious choices we've made in the last several years. Earlier this week, it occurred to us that this particular individual had come an awfully long way in the last year or so. And then we thought — no, maybe it's the country which has come a long way.

President Bill Clinton: When I watched our nation on this journey to reform the health care system, I knew we needed a talented navigator — someone with a rigorous mind, a steady compass, a caring heart. Luckily for me and for our nation, I didn't have to look very far.

Peter Jennings: In politics — even the politics of marriage — it doesn't get any better than this. Public thanks and public confirmation of what so much of the nation knew all along — Hillary Rodham Clinton is anything but just the boss's wife.

Hillary Rodham Clinton: It's been a wonderful experience. I've, you know, worked with my husband, off and on, since we were in law school together, and I'm always excited to do it.

Peter Jennings: Those people who know Hillary Clinton well believe it would have been unthinkable for her to play the traditional wife of a politician. And in these months since the inauguration, up to her neck in trying to reform the health care system, she has been positively liberated.

Henry Grass, Historian: Mrs. Clinton is living proof of what has been developing for a long time — that the presidency is a two-person job at the top.

Peter Jennings: Mrs. Clinton's passion for health care is undeniably deep. She worked tirelessly for healthier children in Arkansas. And her understanding of the health care system was only sharpened earlier this year when her father lay suspended between life and death in a Little Rock hospital. It is the only time she has taken for herself. We have also seen in the last several weeks that this is a woman who understands politics, keeping the naysayers involved in the process, courting her doubters, and winning the respect of even her adversaries.

Senator Connie Mack, (R), Florida: I give Hillary credit for, I think, a tremendous job. She has impressed Democrats and Republicans alike.

Peter Jennings: How long ago it seems that she and her husband were trying just to survive the presidential campaign of a thousand cuts.

Reporter: Do you have any comments about the allegations from Gennifer Flowers?

Peter Jennings: And yet, when the Gennifer Flowers affair threatened to destroy Bill Clinton's campaign, it was Hillary Clinton who told the staff to get on with the job — this was about more than individuals.

Hillary Rodham Clinton: You know, I'm not sitting here as some little woman standing by my man, like Tammy Wynette.

Peter Jennings: And when she appeared to alienate so-called traditional stay at home women — no one was quite sure she had — she apologized and stepped deliberately into her candidate husband's shadow. If this is what it took to win the presidency, this she would do.

Hillary Rodham Clinton: You can do it by making policy or making cookies.

Peter Jennings: The Clintons had no sooner been elected than the nation had its first genuine glimpse of Hillary, the problem solver.

Hillary Rodham Clinton: (voice over) Here is the problem, is that for reasons unknown to us, they opened the gates and let people without tickets in. We just screwed all these people.

Peter Jennings: The power beside the throne, they're saying this week, certainly not behind it. Mrs. Clinton is a very religious, motivated woman determined to make a difference. Listen to a man who has recognized her mission from the time she was young.

Don Jones, Former Youth Minister: I've rarely met a person that has the same kind of burning desire to make the world a better place.

Peter Jennings: As for all the humor about whom is really president?

Hillary Rodham Clinton: As the President said, last night – On behalf of the President — to do what my husband asked me to do.

Peter Jennings: This week, we asked the next generation for some impressions.

First Student: To me, President Clinton is like the actor and Mrs. Clinton is like the director, kind of.

Second Student: She does a lot of what most wives do. I mean, they help out their husbands and like, she's always there to get the milk mustache off of them.

Peter Jennings: However, it turns out, her personal covenant seems to be clear, as she told it to graduating students last spring.

Hillary Rodham Clinton: I have always tried to keep those feelings with me. I want to be idealistic. I want to care about the world. I want to be connected to other people and I hope that you will as well.

Peter Jennings: And so we choose Hillary Rodham Clinton. In 1969, Mrs. Clinton was chosen by her classmates at Wellesley College to be the first student to give a commencement address. She said in that speech that the challenge was to practice politics as the art of making possible what appears to be impossible. In attempting to completely revolutionize the American health care system, she and her husband are attempting just that. That's our report on *World News Tonight*. *20/20* later. I'm Peter Jennings. Have a good weekend and good night.

Announcer: This has been a presentation of ABC News. More Americans get their news from ABC News than from any other source.

TRANSCRIPT 9

PG & E Trains Women
for Construction and "Men's" Jobs

from *World News Tonight*, February 10, 1993

Announcer: From ABC this is *World News Tonight* with Peter Jennings.

Peter Jennings: On the *American Agenda* tonight, making it in a man's world if you're a woman. No question, there have been changes in the American workplace. People don't look twice anymore when they see a woman as doctor or lawyer or business manager, but there are still a great many jobs that men, at least, go on considering men's work. On the *American Agenda* tonight, breaking down another barrier. Our Agenda reporter is Carole Simpson.

1st Woman: I used to go through that, where, "Oh, I'm a woman and I have to do it, and I have to prove myself," but I really don't feel that way anymore.

2nd Woman: You don't have to try and be a man, 'cause chances are a lot of time that works against you.

Felicie Leech: You know that the guys say stuff when you're not there. You always have to be better.

Carole Simpson: This is the toughest battlefield for women fighting sex discrimination and sexual harassment: making it in the male-dominated constructions trades where less than three percent of the jobs are held by women, a figure virtually unchanged since 1980. Sympathetic male co-workers try to explain why other men are so resistant to women.

Clay Lavigne, Foreman: Well, you gotta climb, you know, fall trees and… or you gotta hike up this mountain, and, "Boy, is she physically fit to do this?" Well, that's…their first reaction is, "No, she looks so frail."

Jim Manning, Construction Manager: And these are the type of things that I hear: "Why is she out here working when there's a man that could have that job to support a family?"

Phil Pezzola, Painter: There are still some… some out there that just aren't going to accept it.

Carole Simpson: But many men who work for Pacific Gas and Electric Company in California are learning to accept it. Felicie Leech was in the first big wave of women seeking construction jobs at PG & E in the early 1980s. Today, the former school teacher is a supervisor, teaching apprentice workers, and making twice her old salary. The work is physically demanding and dangerous. [Fel, what's it like up there?]

Felicie Leech: It's wet, cold, but it's okay.

Carole Simpson: Are you scared?

Felicie Leech: You're always scared when you're on a tower.

Carole Simpson: To get where she is today, Felicie said she had to put up with a lot of harassment from men, including pornographic photos in her work area.

Felicie Leech: I think the guys were threatened and operated from fear, and that makes them do pretty crazy things. And when they're together, it's like the, you know, pack mentality.

Carole Simpson: To prevent new female minority employees from being exposed to a hostile workplace, PG & E began a program called Fair Start, a six-week pre-employment training program which prepares them for the demands of work in a non-traditional field. Four hours a day are spent in physical training, especially for strengthening the upper body. The rest of the day, the women are given hands-on training with equipment, tools and safety procedures. Then there is mental preparation….

4th Woman: When you come across some of the guys that have got 20, 25 years, "Well, they never sent me to school."

Carole Simpson: … preparation to work with men who may resent them on the job.

Richard Clarke, Pacific Gas & Electric (PG & E) Chairman: The thing we don't want is to make a special effort to recruit people and then find they can't do the work or do the job. It's devastating to them and it doesn't help the company.

Carole Simpson: The company has also sponsored several committees made up of men and women to help eliminate sexual harassment, which has been one of the major reasons women have quit their jobs.

Jody Aguilar, Construction Worker: If that behavior is bothering you, that is a form of harassment.

Carole Simpson: While there are still problems, the program has been successful in preparing the women for jobs and sensitizing many of the men to the new reality.

Bob Baker, Foreman: It's becoming a work force of not only women, but minorities and everybody else, that we all have to learn to work together.

Carole Simpson: Only 450 women out of PG & E's 6,000 female employees are doing non-traditional work, but the company is making an effort to encourage more women to try it. Clearly, it's not for everybody, but for women like Felicie Leech, it's the most satisfying work she's ever done. [Wouldn't you rather have a desk job?]

Felicie Leech: Not a chance!

Carole Simpson: A fair chance is all these women want. [**Felicie Leech:** All right!] Carole Simpson, ABC News, Santa Rosa, California.

Peter Jennings: That's our report on *World News Tonight*. I'm Peter Jennings. We'll see you tomorrow. Good night.

Announcer: This has been a presentation of ABC News. More American get their news from ABC News than from any other source.

TRANSCRIPT 10

Robert Redford, Sundance Film Festival Founder
from *World News Tonight*, January 29, 1993

Announcer: From ABC this is World News Tonight with Peter Jennings.

Peter Jennings: Finally, this evening, our Person of the Week: – instantly recognizable to millions of people throughout the world, a staple of American culture, and the man we choose this week, because he has become one of the most visible examples of an artist in a fairly selfish industry who believes in giving something back.

Robert Redford: Hollywood's a business. I mean, it makes no mistake about that. And so, therefore, there's a merchant mentality that runs it and there's gonna be more inclination towards formula, you know, towards a guarantee for success. But for those people that have independent vision, you know, special stories to tell, that are more risky, more offbeat, this is the place for them.

Peter Jennings: And Robert Redford welcomes them. They are mostly young filmmakers who've yet to see their name in lights. And this week, eighty-four of them have convened at Redford's Sundance Film Festival in Utah, the biggest in the nation. It is an opportunity to show and promote their work to distributors and producers with money. Most of these films have been produced with very little.

Robert Redford: Some are just horrible. But some are really good and they all take chances. [Film clips from *House of Cards, Into the West, Just Another Girl on the IRT*.] It's about the emergence of new talent, and it's about — for me, I think the most important thing is diversity, which is what I think has been really the engine of our culture and a substantial part of our country's development.

Peter Jennings: Since 1980, Robert Redford has offered hundreds of filmmakers the chance to develop their craft at his Sundance Film Institute in Utah.

Robert Redford: It's a place where people could fail because it's very hard to do that in Hollywood because the meter's ticking. It's costly. I'm old-fashioned, if you want, but I believe in putting something back into an industry that I have taken something out of.

Peter Jennings: Robert Redford, growing up in Los Angeles, was never certain what he wanted to do with his life, but he certainly never calculated that he would be an actor.

Robert Redford: I just kind of fell into it naturally. I started out in art, and art led to the theater, and theater led to film.

Peter Jennings: After his painting career fizzled in Europe — Redford's only sale was just enough to pay his way home — he tried his hand at Broadway. A successful run in Neil Simon's *Barefoot in the Park* in 1963 led him on to some truly forgettable movies, until the film version of *Barefoot in the Park* in 1967 made him a star.

(*Butch Cassidy and the Sundance Kid* scene)

Paul Newman: *I'll jump first.*

Robert Redford: *No.*

Paul Newman: *Then you jump first.*

Robert Redford: *No, I said.*

Paul Newman: *What's the matter with you?*

Robert Redford: *I can't swim.*

Peter Jennings: In the 1970s, he was in hit after hit: *Butch Cassidy and the Sundance Kid* with Paul Newman; *The Way We Were* with Barbra Streisand; *The Sting*.

(*The Sting* scene)

First Actor: *Got a system?*

Robert Redford: *No. You can still lose with a system.*

(*All the President's Men* scene)

Robert Redford: *Can you confirm it?*

Dustin Hoffman: *Absolutely.*

Peter Jennings: And with Dustin Hoffman in *All the President's Men* — how Richard Nixon fell as a result of Watergate.

(*All the President's Men* scene)

Robert Redford: *Bernstein got another source.*

Dustin Hoffman: *The guy at Justice confirmed.*

Jason Robards: *If there's any doubt, we can run it tomorrow.*

Robert Redford: *You don't have to. The story's solid. We're sure of it.*

Peter Jennings: By the mid-1970s, Redford, now a major star, began to apply his considerable fame and clout to a cause.

Robert Redford: The United States is far behind in its realization of solar energy as a …

Peter Jennings: He put his talent and his money into protecting the environment.

Robert Redford: *The grandeur of the scene was softened by haze over the valley.*

Peter Jennings: Redford continued to make commercial movies in the 1980's. His only regret, he says, is that unlike the character he played in *The Natural*, he cannot hit a baseball like Ted Williams.

Robert Redford: When he hit a baseball, I said that's what I'd like to do. I didn't. I made a movie of it.

(*Sneakers* scene)

Robert Redford: *Sorry to waste your time, gentlemen. I don't work for the government.*

Peter Jennings: Redford is 55 now. He continues to make movies fairly regularly, and he continues to use his name and his financial resources so that others can do the same.

Robert Redford: The most satisfying to me is - the thing that is my main course, which is the art of film. That's the most important because that's what I do.

Peter Jennings: And so we choose Robert Redford because he believes in the newcomers, which means he believes in the future. That's our report on *World News Tonight*. I'm Peter Jennings. *20/20* later. We'll see you on Monday. Good night.

TRANSCRIPT 11

TV Technology

from *World News Tonight*, September 28, 1993

Announcer: From ABC this is *World News Tonight* with Peter Jennings.

Peter Jennings: On the *American Agenda* tonight, the revolution in your living room. Most all of us who watch television — not to mention those of us who work in it — have at least the sense that the whole television universe is shifting under our feet. On this broadcast, for example, we sometimes wonder not how, but where we will fit in the new world of 500 channels. And we're as confused as anyone. So we asked our media analyst, Jeff Greenfield, to spend the next three nights guiding us down this new information superhighway so that we may know better how to tune in tomorrow.

Jeff Greenfield, ABC News: We don't always know what the future is going to look like. In 1939, this is what they thought 1960 would be like.

1st Documentary Narrator: *On many of the buildings are landing decks for helicopters and auto gyros.*

Jeff Greenfield: In 1964, they thought we'd be living like this by now.

2nd Documentary Narrator: *Vehicles, electronically paced, travel routes remarkably safe, swift, and efficient.*

Jeff Greenfield: But when it comes to the most commonly shared experience in American life — watching television — there's no doubt that the future is not just around the corner, but knocking on the front door. Television is about to be literally reinvented — a reinvention of enormous significance.

Mitch Kapor, Electronic Frontier Foundation: Over a generation I think it's going

142

to be as important as the television and the telephone were.

Rep. Ed Markey, House Telecommunications: The decisions which we're making right now will, to a very large extent, shape the identity of the United States as an economy and as a people.

Jeff Greenfield: At first it may not look like much of a revolution, just a lot more of the same. Cable customers in parts of New York are already wired for 150 channels. And within a few years, 500 channel systems will be commonplace. And so will cable channels aimed at ever narrower tastes. At that rate, if you spend five seconds looking at each channel, it would take you more than forty minutes just to surf through a 500 channel system. But that's not what is coming. This is television you can really talk back to.

Randy: Hi, Jack.

Jack: Hi, Randy. How are you doing tonight?

Randy: Pretty good.

Jeff Greenfield: The real story is that the whole nature of television is changing from a one-way communication system to a world where you tell your TV set what you want to see, when you want to see it.

Viewer: Let's see what's available the third of October.

Jeff Greenfield: And this is the heart of the revolution — a cable of optic fibers so efficient that one strand can transmit the entire *Encyclopedia Britannica* in one second. It can move pictures, sound, and data, back and forth. And that's the key — back and forth.

What's happening now is that the features of cable TV, the telephone, and the computer, are all converging into one device — one that makes it possible to tap into an apparently limitless universe of entertainment and information, a universe where today's couch potato is tomorrow's navigator.

Author George Gilder was one of the first to see just how big a change is coming.

George Gilder, Discovery Institute: Just as you can pick up the telephone today and call anybody you want on the face of the Earth, you'll be able to dial up any database, theater, library, church, any university classroom.

Jeff Greenfield: A hint of what is coming can be seen right now on Montreal's Videoway system. Viewers watching a baseball game can push a button on their remote control and call up a player's statistics, even his salary.

And some cable systems are already trying out video on demand. You tell your TV set what kind of TV show or movie you want to see, you preview it, and order and pay for it with a click of your remote control.

You can play a high-tech video game with a friend across town or across the country. And home shopping will become something more than watching cubic zirconiums float by. It will mean calling up what you want to shop for, examining the goods, and ordering them.

More significant — as cable and phone companies battle to build this information superhighway, the possibility of ordering up books or health records, or receiving and sending work from the home, starts to become much

143

more than a pipe dream.

Vice President Gore has been a leading advocate for the information superhighway for years.

Vice President Al Gore: I want to see a time when a school child can come home after class, and instead of playing a video game, plug into the Library of Congress and explore a whole universe of information, not in terms of words alone, but in terms of vivid color moving pictures that respond to that child's imagination. Why not? We know how to do it technologically.

Jeff Greenfield: But there's also a lot we don't know. How much interactivity do viewers really want? How much is it going to cost? Who gets to build and control this information superhighway? And what happens to those who can't afford to ride it?

Jeff Greenfield, ABC News, New York.

Peter Jennings: That's our report on *World News Tonight*. I'm Peter Jennings. See you tomorrow.

Announcer: This has been a presentation of ABC News. More Americans get their news from ABC News than from any other source.

TRANSCRIPT 12

What's Become of Hollywood?
from *Nightline*, March 28, 1989

Ethel Merman: *There's no business /like show business /like no business I know.*

Forrest Sawyer: Hollywood in its heyday: big stars, big studios, big productions, America's dream factory.

Ethel Merman: *Nowhere could you get that happy feeling /when you are stealing that extra bow.*

Forrest Sawyer: There's no business like show business.

Ethel Merman: *There's no people like show people/ they smile when they are low.*

Forrest Sawyer: But behind the glamour are accountants and corporate conglomerates. With money men calling the shots, what's become of the movie makers of old?

Ethel Merman: *Let's go on with the show.*

Announcer: This is ABC News *Nightline*. Substituting for Ted Koppel and reporting from New York, Forrest Sawyer.

Forrest Sawyer: Back in 1908, when a bunch of unruly wildcatters decided to make southern California home for the unheard-of business of filmmaking, local residents were appalled. In fact, the Hollywood Hotel stuck out a sign that read, "No dogs and no actors allowed."

But to everyone's amazement, the wildcatters struck oil, and Hollywood was transformed from a sleepy suburb to the dream capital of the world. An industry that started out offering two features for a penny, last year took in 4 and a half billion dollars at the box office. It is big business now, but it's still a business for wildcatters. Only one script in a thousand is made into a movie, and only 40 percent of those movies make any profit at all. What's the movie business really like? Judd Rose begins our report with a visit to the land where dreams are high-stakes gambles.

Judd Rose, ABC News: In Hollywood, the land of the myth-makers, the greatest myth they ever made was their own.

Director: (voice-over) Quiet. Camera. Action.

Actor (Hollywood Hotel scene, Turner Program Services): *Hooray for Hollywood! /That screwy ballyhooey Hollywood /where any office boy or young mechanic /can be a panic /with just a good-looking pan.*

Actress: *And any shopgirl /can be a top girl /if she pleases a tired businessman.*

Judd Rose: The Hollywood myth was simply the American dream draped with tinsel. It didn't matter who you were, anyone could be a star. Waiting in the west was a land of glamour and beauty, and fantasy factories that spun more tales than Scheherazade.

Kathryn Grayson (Showboat scene, MGM): *We could make believe I loved you.*

Judd Rose: Today, where the showboat once docked, there's a parking lot.

Gene Kelly (Singin' in the Rain scene, MGM): *I'm singin' in the rain, just singin' in the rain …*

Judd Rose: Where Gene Kelly went singin' in the rain, there's now a retirement home. The giant sound stage where Esther Williams danced on water is empty now; the huge pool has been sealed over. Even Schwab's drugstore where, legend has it, Lana Turner was discovered, will soon be a shopping mall.

Vivien Leigh (Gone With The Wind scene, MGM): *As God is my witness, I'll never be hungry again.*

Judd Rose: 50 years ago, MGM gave us *Gone With the Wind*. A film classic, it won eight Academy Awards. This year, MGM has a different sort of classic. *Rain Man*, nominated for eight Oscars, is expected to win most of Hollywood's top honors tomorrow night.

But even with the success of *Rain Man*, MGM, once king of this jungle, is now a weak kitten. The fabled Metro lot belongs to Lorimar Telepictures, which recently merged with Warner Brothers, which soon may merge with Time, Incorporated. MGM has moved to offices across the street, where it now exists mainly on paper, run by an investment banker.

Well, Louis B. Mayer is long gone. MGM is now owned by a shrewd tycoon named Kirk Kirkorian. A few years ago, he sold it to Ted Turner, who grabbed the valuable film library for his TV network, and then sold it right back. Well, since then, Kirkorian has stripped off almost all the remaining assets and now he's asking about a billion and a half dollars to sell what's left. All, that is, except MGM's famous trademark, the roaring lion. He says he'll keep that.

Alex Ben Block, Journalist: It's a financial shell game in which Kirk Kirkorian is moving the pieces around for his profit. It's perfectly legal, but there's something that makes me feel it's slightly immoral.

Judd Rose: It's called show business, and it's always been just that, a business, but never before has the bottom line been such a top priority.

Jon Peters, Producer: The average price of a picture today could be $18 or $20 million, and then when you put up prints and ads, that's another $10 or $15 million. That's a $35 million investment, and with interest, that's a very big investment, because there are no guarantees in our business.

Judd Rose: As Jon Peters and Peter Guber know well. In recent years they've produced hits like *Rain Man*, *The Color Purple*, and *Flashdance*. They've also produced expensive box-office flops, like *Inner Space* and *Gorillas in the Mist*. Now their hopes are riding on *Batman*.

(*Batman*, Guber-Peters Ent. Co. scene)

Actor: *What kind of a world we live in where a man dressed us as a bat …*

Judd Rose: *Batman* is expected to be Warner Brothers' summer blockbuster, among a coming glut of big summer movies.

Jon Peters: We can build it up in here. Build the tension.

(*Batman* scene)

Actor: *The villian is truly mightier than the sword.*

Judd Rose: The rule of thumb is, a film has to make at least three times its production cost just to break even, and *Batman* cost more than $30 million. So Peters and Guber are keeping a close eye on everything, from the trailers to the posters.

Graphic Designer: Basically, we want to be very audacious. We want to have a very simple poster, no Keaton, no Nicholson, be audacious, burn in the logo, get the logo established. It's the color of the movie.

Jon Peters: I love it.

Peter Gruber, Producer: He loves it.

Jon Peters: I love the shape, I love the way it looks like it's almost flying, and I love, actually, that it's the batwing.

Graphic Designer: And it has a little edge, it looks a little dangerous.

Jon Peters: Yeah.

Judd Rose: *Batman* looks like a hit, but then, so did *Howard the Duck*.

Peter Guber: It's not a predictive science, you know. Sometimes you put the same ingredients together, and you leave them in the oven, and it turns out to be chocolate pudding. Another time it's soufflé. And the person who says, "I know it's a hit," you're looking at a fool.

Judd Rose: In Hollywood, a fool and his Rolls are soon parted, so the big studios want sure things. If it works once, try it again—and again. That's why you saw *Baby Boom*, and *Three Men and a Baby*, and *She's Having a Baby*. That's why there are so many sequels, like *Lethal Weapon 2*, *Indiana Jones III*, *Star Trek V*. This year alone, there will be as many as thirty sequels. Hollywood, in short, likes to play it safe.

David Puttnam, Former President, Columbia Pictures: The studio's job is to protect themselves and to make money. It's the filmmakers job to get fine films on the screen. At some point in the last 15 years, I think that we as filmmakers began to lose our way, and it's we who are failing, not the studios. The studios aren't failing at all.

Judd Rose: A surprising sentiment coming from David Puttnam. The respected producer of *Chariots of Fire* Puttnam was made head of Columbia Pictures, and in his quest for quality, he went to war with top stars, big producers, and powerful agents.

David Puttnam: Power brings with it enormous responsibility. And if the agents are as powerful as I believe they are, and I'm prepared to accept they are, then the movies should be getting better, because the role of the agents is to represent the creative sector. By general consensus, I think you'll find everyone in the industry feels, me included, that the films are disappointing.

Judd Rose: *Ghostbusters* was a huge hit for Columbia, and a sequel was planned. But Puttnam refused to give in to the extravagant salary demands and the deal making needed to get done. Puttnam was fired after less than a year. *Ghostbusters 2* hits the theaters this June.

Seen any good movies lately?

David Puttnam: Not as many as I'd like to.

Forrest Sawyer: And that is our report for tonight. I'm Forrest Sawyer in New York. For all of us here at ABC News. Good night.

Announcer: This has been a presentation of ABC News. Where more Americans get their news than from any other source.
